BATTLEGROUND

1916 In Focus

Battleground

The Battle for the General Post Office, 1916

Paul O'Brien

NEW ISLAND

BATTLEGROUND
First published in 2015
by New Island Books
16 Priory Office Park
Stillorgan
Co. Dublin
Republic of Ireland

www.newisland.ie

Copyright © Paul O'Brien, 2015

The author has asserted his moral rights.

Print ISBN: 978-1-84840-427-4
Epub ISBN: 978-1-84840-448-9
Mobi ISBN: 978-1-84840-449-6

British Library Cataloguing Data.
A CIP catalogue record for this book is available from the British Library.

Typeset by JVR Creative India
Cover Design by Mariel Deegan
Printed by ScandBook AB, Sweden

The revolution is not a social dinner,
a literary event,
a drawing or an embroidery;
it cannot be done with elegance and courtesy.
The revolution is an act of violence.

Mao Tse-Tung

A Noblett's
B The Arch
C Lawrence's toy shop
D Tyler's Boots
E Arnott & Co. Ltd. Drapers
F Bewley Sons & Co.
G Coliseum Variety Theatre
H MacInerney & Co. and Imperial Hotel
I *General Post Office*
J Clery & Co. and Imperial Hotel
K True Form Boot Co.
L Freeman's Journal
M Hotel Metropole
N Eason & Son Ltd. Newsagents
O Mansfield Boot - Makers
P Hoyte & Son
Q Hibernian Bank
R Reis and Co.
S Wynne's Hotel
T D.B.C. Restaurant
U Hopkins & Hopkins
V Kelly's Fort

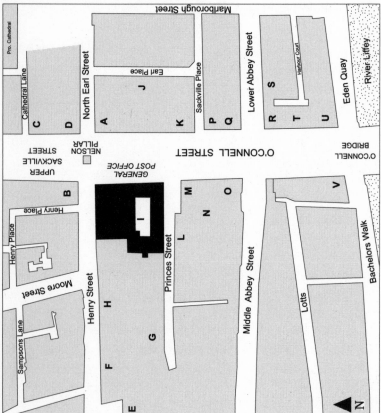

Contents

Acknowledgements   ix

The Proclamation of the Irish Republic 1916   xi

Foreword   1

1. Easter Monday, 24 April 1916: Morning   7

2. Easter Monday, 24 April 1916: GHQ   15

3. Easter Monday, 24 April 1916: Afternoon   21

4. Easter Monday, 24 April 1916: Defensive Posts   30

5. Easter Monday, 24 April 1916: Evening   37

6. Tuesday, 25 April 1916: FOB Trinity   43

7. Wednesday, 26 April 1916: Hold and Secure   50

8. Wednesday, 26 April 1916: No Man's Land   57

9. Thursday, 27 April 1916: Morning   66

10. Thursday, 27 April 1916: Afternoon   71

11. Thursday, 27 April 1916: Evening   78

12. Friday, 28 April 1916: Morning   84

13. Friday, 28 April 1916: Afternoon   92

14. Friday, 28 April 1916: Evening   99

15. Saturday, 29 April 1916: The Last Stand   107

16. Trial and Error   115

17. Military Success and Military Failure   121

Conclusion   127

Endnotes   129

Select Bibliography   135

Index   137

Acknowledgements

Sackville Street, now known as O'Connell Street, has and still does witness some of the most momentous occasions in Irish history. During the 1916 Rising, the streetscape was devastated by artillery fire. The urban battlefield in which the Irish Volunteers and the British army found themselves fighting is still there, hidden away in the lanes and alleyways that surround the General Post Office. This work retells some of the many engagements that took place in this area of operations during Easter week, 1916.

Grateful thanks are once again due to the staff of the National Library (Dublin), the National Archives, the Military Archives (Dublin), the Kilmainham Gaol Archives and the staff of the Sherwood Forester Museum. A special word of thanks to Nuala Canny of the OPW Library, who provided expertise in finding books that proved invaluable.

I am indebted to Sue Sutton and Roger E. Nixon for their research in the British military archives at Kew in London; to Gerry Woods for cartography and to Andrew D. Hesketh and Dr Mike Briggs for material on the Sherwood Foresters.

For supporting the idea and reading the initial drafts, a special word of thanks to Dr Mary Montaut, John McGuiggan and Sgt Wayne Fitzgerald.

I would like to thank the following people for their insight, support and encouragement: Eoin Purcell, Henry Fairbrother, Ronnie Daly, David Kilmartin, the staff at *An Cosantóir*, Joe Kinnear, Joe Malone, Irish Regiments, Eamon Bohan, Kieran Delany, Dave and Jimmy Smith and Jason Nolan.

I am indebted to Liz Gillis, Las Fallon, Micheál O Doibhlín, James Langton and Ray Bateson, extraordinary historians who were most generous with their time in providing information and answering questions.

I would like to thank all the staff at New Island Books, in particular Daniel Bolger, whose perceptive editing has made such a difference.

Many thanks are due to my parents, Thomas and Rita O'Brien, for their continued support.

And nearly last, but in almost every way first, I want to thank my wife Marian for her truly bottomless love, patience, support, counsel and cheer. This book could not have been possible without her. She is, in every way, a partner and a soulmate.

There are many people who helped with this book and in naming some of them I can only apologise to those I fear I may have indirectly forgotten and I would like to invite them to make me aware of any omissions or relevant information that may be included in any future updated edition.

Paul O'Brien
April 2015
paulobrienauthor.ie

The Proclamation of the Irish Republic 1916

IRISHMEN AND IRISHWOMEN: In the name of God and of the dead generations from which she receives her old tradition of nationhood, Ireland, through us, summons her children to her flag and strikes for her freedom.

Having organised and trained her manhood through her secret revolutionary organisation, the Irish Republican Brotherhood, and through her open military organisations, the Irish Volunteers and the Irish Citizen Army, having patiently perfected her discipline, having resolutely waited for the right moment to reveal itself, she now seizes that moment, and supported by her exiled children in America and by gallant allies in Europe, but relying in the first on her own strength, she strikes in full confidence of victory.

We declare the right of the people of Ireland to the ownership of Ireland and to unfettered control of Irish destinies, to be sovereign and indefeasible. The long usurpation of that right by a foreign people and government has not extinguished the right, nor can it ever be extinguished except by the destruction of the Irish people. In every generation the Irish people have asserted their right to national freedom and sovereignty; six times during the past three hundred years they have asserted it in arms. Standing on that fundamental right and again asserting it in arms in the face of the world, we hereby proclaim the Irish Republic as a Sovereign Independent State, and we pledge our lives and the lives of our comrades in arms to the cause of its freedom, of its welfare, and of its exaltation among the nations.

The Irish Republic is entitled to, and hereby claims, the allegiance of every Irishman and Irishwoman. The Republic guarantees religious and civil liberty, equal rights and equal opportunities to all its citizens and declares its resolve to pursue the happiness and prosperity of the whole nation and of all its parts, cherishing all of the children of the nation equally, and oblivious of the differences carefully fostered by an alien government, which have divided a minority from the majority in the past.

Until our arms have brought the opportune moment for the establishment of a permanent National Government, representative of the whole people of Ireland and elected by the suffrages of all her men and women, the Provisional Government, hereby constituted, will administer the civil and military affairs of the Republic in trust for the people.

We place the cause of the Irish Republic under the protection of the Most High God, Whose blessing we invoke upon our arms, and we pray that no one who serves that cause will dishonour it by cowardice, inhumanity, or rapine. In this supreme hour the Irish nation must, by its valour and discipline, and by the readiness of its children to sacrifice themselves for the common good, prove itself worthy of the august destiny to which it is called.

Battleground

Signed on behalf of the Provisional Government:

Thomas J. Clarke

Seán Mac Diarmada.	Thomas MacDonagh.
P. H. Pearse.	Eamonn Ceannt.
James Connolly.	Joseph Plunkett.

Foreword

The most iconic building in Ireland is the General Post Office (GPO), which is located on Dublin city's main thoroughfare, O'Connell Street. In 1916, this building was designated as both the civil and military headquarters of the Irish Republican Army as it attempted to overthrow British rule in Ireland.

Designed by Francis Johnson and opened to the public in 1818, the original General Post Office was classical in design and measured 200ft long and 150ft wide. Constructed from mountain granite with a portico of Portland stone, the building stood 50ft in height and was divided into three storeys. Its six fluted ionic columns supported a pediment surmounted by statues of Mercury, Fidelity and Hibernia that were designed by John Smyth.

The building housed an important central civil service department that catered for postal, banking and, by 1916, telephone and telegraph facilities. In 1912, Hamilton Norway was appointed Secretary of the Post Office and immediately began refurbishing the building in order to make it befitting of the second city of the British Empire.

Mary Louisa Norway, wife of Hamilton, wrote:

It was really beautiful. The roof was a large glass dome, with elaborate plaster work, beautiful white pillars, mosaic floor, counters all of red teak wood and bright brass fittings everywhere – a public building of which any city might be proud.[1]

Unlike the GPO, however, the rest of the city was in steady decline. Enclosed within two canals, the Royal to the north of the city and the Grand to the south, Dublin was divided by the River Liffey, with its quays and several bridges linking the north to the south. On the city's main thoroughfare, Sackville Street (now O'Connell Street), stood two statues, one of Daniel O'Connell and the other of Charles Stewart Parnell, both symbols of the advances made in the previous century towards constitutional nationalism. However, in the centre of the street the 134ft Nelson's Pillar dominated the skyline, a figure of British imperialism gazing out over the city's inhabitants. Behind Sackville Street's façade of commercial respectability, there lurked another world, hidden in the warren of alleyways and lanes. Many of the once-magnificent Georgian buildings had become tenements, with Dublin's poor living in appalling, squalid conditions flanked by one of Europe's largest red light districts, Monto.

In April 1916, a relatively small but determined group of Irish men and women took Britain's conflict with Germany during the First World War as an opportunity to strike a blow for Irish independence.

As it was possible that Home Rule would be implemented, many northern Protestants formed the Ulster Volunteer Force (UVF) to defend Britain's union with Ireland. In response to this action, Irish nationalists formed the Irish Volunteers in November 1913. The Irish Citizen Army (ICA), under the command of labour leader James Connolly, was a paramilitary offshoot of the militant labour union, the Irish Transport and General Workers' Union, formed primarily to defend union members during the 1913 Lockout. A threatened civil war between the UVF, the Irish Volunteers and the British government was averted with the outbreak of the First World War in August 1914. The Irish Republican Brotherhood (IRB) set about planning a rising against British rule in Ireland and made contact with Germany in order to acquire munitions and manpower. The leaders of both the Volunteers and the ICA believed that a combined force would have more success and in early 1916 an alliance was formed.

The Supreme Council of the IRB fixed the date for the Rising as Sunday, 23 April 1916. Eoin MacNeill, Chief of Staff of the Irish Volunteers, withdrew his support for the Rising, having heard that Roger Casement had been arrested and that the *Aud,* a German ship laden with arms and ammunition, had been intercepted by the Royal Navy. MacNeill issued a countermanding order, cancelling the mobilisation of republican forces, which was published in the national press and distributed by couriers throughout the country.

The Military Council of the IRB decided, however, to go ahead with the Rising despite MacNeill's order and rescheduled the insurrection for the following day, Monday, 24 April 1916.

While republican battalions occupied a number of positions in Dublin, the area of operations for the Battalion headquarters of the Irish Republican Army was to be Sackville Street (now O'Connell Street) and the surrounding area, with the centrally located General Post Office designated as General Headquarters (GHQ).

The battle for the General Post Office in Sackville Street is seen by many as an epic struggle against one of the largest military forces in the world. Hundreds of people would die and thousands would be injured as British troops fought to regain control of the metropolis, a struggle that would see the city reduced to rubble.

The 1916 Rising was a seminal event in the history of twentieth-century Ireland. It was regarded by republicans, then and since, as a glorious fight for emancipation, a major step on the path towards an independent Ireland. Others saw it as a betrayal at a time when Britain was at war.

The battle for the GPO poses a number of questions for the student of military history in relation to the strategy employed by British forces. Having identified the GPO as the insurgents' headquarters, General W. H. M. Lowe manoeuvred his troops into position within three days for an all-out attack on the building. The tactics employed in order to retake the capital involved his men fighting it out with the enemy in an agonising block-by-block struggle, an action that would endanger the population and destroy the centre of the city.

With regard to the Irish side, questions arise in relation to Joseph Plunkett's and James Connolly's strategy. The failure of the insurgent forces to capture Trinity College and secure Dame Street enabled the military to establish a central base that severed the Volunteer communication lines, leaving the GPO isolated. Controversy surrounds Plunkett's and Connolly's plan of occupying and holding positions in the city in the hope that the general population would rise in support – an act which never came about. The decision by Volunteer command to rise on Easter Monday, 24 April 1916 with a force that was seriously under strength due to Eoin MacNeill's countermanding order must also be questioned, as must their failure to consider the possible use of artillery against their republican positions, which left the insurrection destined to fail.

The Rising has been analysed by academics and historians, commemorated in songs and ballads, and variously revered and reviled. While there has been disagreement regarding its effects and results, there can be no doubt about its central place in the history of modern Ireland. The Easter Rising of 1916 and the War of Independence that followed had a profound influence on the shaping of modern Ireland. The great swing in public opinion that brought about these changes can only be explained in the context of 1916 and its impact on Ireland and its people.

While many books have been written on the Rising and those who participated in it, this work is purely an attempt to detail the actions in the area of operations 'in and around' the General Post Office. The newly proclaimed Irish Republic was quickly and brutally suppressed, but the heroism demonstrated that week and the executions that followed changed Irish history forever. What follows is the story of 1916 and the battle for the General Post Office.

Chapter 1

Easter Monday,
24 April 1916: Morning

CHARGE!

At 08.00 hours on Monday, 24 April 1916, Liberty Hall, the headquarters of the Irish Citizen Army at Beresford Place, was a hive of activity. Armed guards stood to attention at the main door of the premises, allowing entrance only to the countless couriers that came and went from the building with great urgency. Sandbags festooned the windows and a small armed picquet of men stood guard in case there was an attempt to attack the building.

Throughout the morning, members of the Irish Citizen Army, Cumann na mBán, Fianna Éireann and the Irish Volunteers mobilised at Liberty Hall to await further orders. Following the capture of the German ammunition ship, the *Aud*, and MacNeill's countermanding order, Volunteer mobilisation throughout the country had been incomplete.

The Military Council of the IRB had sent out messengers to the various battalions across the country rescheduling the insurrection for noon on the Easter Bank Holiday Monday, 24

April 1916. Confusion reigned amongst the rank and file of the various republican organisations, resulting in many refusing or ignoring the order to mobilise on the Monday. The turnout for those Companies that did mobilise in rural areas was small and many returned home, presuming that the Rising would not go ahead.

Many members of the Irish Citizen Army, anticipating some form of action, had slept in Liberty Hall overnight and others had arrived in the early hours of the morning. Corridors were filled with men and women dressed in an array of clothing and military accoutrements, waiting for something to happen. Helena Molony of the ICA recalls:

> The [Citizen Army] women had no uniform, in the ordinary sense, nor the men either. Some of the men had green coats. They wore an ordinary slouch hat, like the Boer hat, and mostly a belt. They insisted they were citizen soldiers, not military soldiers – at the same time regimented and disciplined. I had an Irish tweed costume, with a Sam Browne [military belt]. I had my own revolver and ammunition.[1]

Many Volunteers were dressed in their grey-green uniforms with puttees, water bottles and haversacks. Others wore their everyday clothes criss-crossed with ammunition bandoliers. They were armed with a variety of weapons, including rifles, revolvers, shotguns and automatic pistols.

Those Volunteers who would make up the Headquarters Battalion to occupy the General Post Office (I) on Sackville Street were drawn from the four city battalions, the Irish

Citizen Army and the Kimmage Volunteers. Among the latter group, some had evaded conscription in Britain while others were on the run in Ireland for nationalist activities. This group, commanded by George Plunkett and Frank Thornton, numbered seventy-five members and was loosely attached to the 4th Battalion. It took the name 'Pearse's Own' but was more commonly known as the 'Kimmage Garrison' or the 'London Irish'. In total there were only 150 men available to seize and hold the building on Dublin's main thoroughfare.

In an attic room within Liberty Hall, the General Headquarters staff were assembling.

The Headquarters Battalion was to be led to the GPO by James Connolly, Commandant General of the Dublin Division of the newly formed Irish Republican Army and signatory of the Proclamation of the Irish Republic. Connolly, an ardent socialist and union official, had formed the Irish Citizen Army during the turbulent period of the 1913 Lockout. The amalgamation of his force and the Irish Volunteers had resulted in his new command.

On a table ready for collection were a number of copies of the Proclamation of the Irish Republic that had been printed over the weekend. These were handed to a junior officer for safe keeping. The Proclamation had been signed by Connolly and six others: Patrick Pearse, Thomas Clarke, Seán Mac Diarmada, Thomas MacDonagh, Eamonn Ceannt and Joseph Plunkett, some of whom were in the cramped and dimly lit attic room.

Patrick Pearse, who held the rank of Commander-in-Chief of the Army of the Republic and President of the Provisional Government, was also a poet, writer, educationalist, lawyer and revolutionary. A member of the Military Council of the IRB, he had helped plan the Rising. His younger brother, William, was also in attendance, as he was assigned to his older brother's staff as his personal attaché.

Seated on a chair was Thomas Clarke, who was the first of the seven signatories to sign the Proclamation. Clarke had spent many years in prison for Fenian activities and was responsible for reorganising the IRB. He was also responsible for establishing the secret Military Council of the IRB. Seán Mac Diarmada, a native of County Leitrim, was a member of the Military Council. He stood nearby, supported by his walking cane, having suffered from polio four years earlier.

Outside, Joseph Plunkett arrived by cab accompanied by two officers, his aide-de-camp, Michael Collins, and W. J. Brennan Whitmore. Plunkett held the post of Director of Military Operations and was responsible, along with Connolly, for the military planning of the Rising. He had suffered from bad health throughout his life and was weak due to having recently undergone an operation for glandular tuberculosis. As he exited the cab and made his way into Liberty Hall, the officers received a general salute. Once inside, the officers made their way upstairs to the small attic room where they were greeted by the other members of the Military Council. The only signatories absent were Commandant Eamonn Ceannt and Commandant Thomas MacDonagh. Ceannt was commanding the 4th Battalion in the field and was at that moment taking up position within the South Dublin Union.[2] MacDonagh was occupying Jacob's Biscuit Factory with elements of the 2nd Battalion.

After a brief conversation, the group of officers descended the staircase and proceeded to make their way outside. As the officers appeared outside the building, Volunteer Joe Good described their attire:

> I remember seeing Joe Plunkett with plans in his hand outside Liberty Hall. He was beautifully dressed, having high tan leather boots, spurs, pince-nez and looked like any British brass hat staff officer.
>
> Connolly looked drab beside him in a bottle green thin serge uniform. The form of dress of the two men impressed me as representing two different ideas of freedom.[3]

In order to give Commandant Edward Daly's 1st Battalion time to occupy and secure the Four Courts and the surrounding area, Connolly issued Captain Séan Heuston the following order:

> Take the Mendicity Institute today at 12 o'clock at all costs.
>
> Signed J. Connolly.[4]

A small rearguard was to remain at Liberty Hall in order to convey the remainder of the ammunition and supplies to Battalion headquarters later that day.

A motor car, laden with weapons, appeared on the quay corner driven by the O'Rahilly, a native of County Kerry. He insisted on being called 'The O'Rahilly', which was the title used for the head of the old Irish O'Rahilly clan. Having driven the previous day to County Limerick issuing MacNeill's countermanding order, the O'Rahilly made his way to Liberty Hall, having learned that his comrades were 'going out'. A great cheer went up from the assembled soldiers as the car came to a halt and the O'Rahilly dismounted and entered the hall.

At 11.30 hours, an officer appeared on the steps and called on the men to form ranks. A horse-drawn lorry laden with an assortment of weapons, ammunition boxes and labourers' implements such as crowbars, sledgehammers and pickaxes appeared on the street. Séamus Robinson of the Kimmage Garrison wrote:

> Beresford Place was full of Citizen Army men and women. Everything was bustle and excitement. We formed up in front of, and [with] our backs to, Liberty Hall, and Margaret Skinnider, whom I knew, rushed over to me and said, 'It's on.' I asked, 'What's on?' She said, 'The rebellion, of course.' This was the first positive information I had that action was to be taken that morning.[5]

Senior officers assembled on the steps of Liberty Hall and viewed their men. James Connolly addressed two platoons under the commands of Captain Seán Connolly and Commandant Michael Mallin, which moved off towards Dublin Castle and St Stephen's Green.[6]

Many of those assembled now realised the seriousness of the tasks ahead. Jim O'Shea of the Irish Citizen Army later recalled that:

> It was moving to 11.30 a.m. and we each had our own thoughts and little things that never mattered before came up in our minds. Home, people, friends and the chances of the fight, what it would be like being killed,

what of the next world? Those remote things that never gave you a thought before seemed important at the moment. It did not fill you with sorrow or foreboding, only an abstract removal from realities ...[7]

At 11.50 hours the final column of men prepared to move out. As the order 'By the left, quick march' was given, the column moved off to a rousing cheer from onlookers. Connolly led the procession with Pearse taking up position near the head of the troop. Unsheathing his sword and discarding the scabbard, General Joseph Plunkett, assisted by his aide-de-camp Michael Collins, joined the ranks. The only female in the group was Connolly's personal secretary, Winnie Carney, who carried her typewriter and a service revolver.

Moving off at a brisk pace, the procession marched up Eden Quay towards Sackville Street before swinging onto Lower Abbey Street. They avoided the main thoroughfares in an effort to evade interception by the Crown forces. On reaching the junction of Lower Abbey Street and Sackville Street, a section under Peader Bracken and Seamus Robinson detached itself from the column and moved towards the bridge. Their mission was to 'over watch' on the bridge and provide covering fire if there were any attempts by enemy forces to interfere with the column.

The main column turned right onto Sackville Street and continued their march towards the GPO.

As 2nd Lieutenant A. D. Chalmers of the 14th Royal Fusiliers walked past the Metropole Hotel (M) on Sackville Street, he noticed his fellow British officers standing in the doorway of the hotel eying the Volunteer troop with contempt.

As he crossed the road towards the GPO, Chalmers remarked to a friend, 'Just look at that awful crowd, they must be on a route march.'[8]

As the Volunteer column came abreast of the GPO (I), the command rang out, 'Company halt, left turn.' Connolly then bellowed out the command, 'The GPO, charge!' The 1916 Easter Rising had commenced.

Chapter 2

Easter Monday,
24 APRIL 1916: GHQ

At 12.05 hours, the Volunteers rushed through the main entrance into the building firing a salvo of revolver shots into the air. Panic gripped those inside as Connolly ordered all civilians to leave the building immediately. While many people ran to the exits, others had to be persuaded at the point of a bayonet. Lieutenant Chalmers, who had entered the General Post Office only moments before, soon found himself facing a loaded revolver and a pike. Michael Collins grabbed the unfortunate officer and tied him up with a telephone cable before thrusting him into a telephone booth.

Some of the postal workers stood outside, bewildered by the series of events which had just occurred. Regaining their composure, they moved down Talbot Street towards the nearest railway station where they proceeded to set up an emergency telegraph and telephone line to London. Samuel Gutherie telephoned the superintendent on duty in the Central Telegraph Office in London and said:

I am speaking from Amiens St. RI. The GPO has been taken possession of by the Irish Volunteers who have turned out everyone.

I am afraid they are bent on demolishing the instrument room. I tell you in case you have wondered why you cd not get DN. Will you please advise Secretary & anyone else that it may concern & also advise Irish Stns [?you] may be right to. Yes I will take Govt work and will do best to deliver it. *The streets are not safe.*[1]

Within the General Post Office (I), Commandant General Connolly stood in the centre of the hall and shouted, 'Smash those windows, and fortify them, and barricade the doors!' Glass shattered out onto the street as rifle butts smashed the windowpanes. Barricades of ledgers, books, pads of money orders, telegram pads, files and furniture were placed against the windowsills; the tables were pushed against the walls to make improvised firing steps. Volunteers were ordered to fill mailbags with coal from the cellar and place them at the windows as barricades.

A squad moved to the yard at the rear of the building where they secured the van entrance, admitting the horse-drawn dray and the O'Rahilly's car, both vehicles laden with supplies and weapons. An ammunition dump containing an array of firearms and edged weapons was set up behind the main office. Large stocks of homemade grenades were distributed throughout the building. These grenades were constructed from tin cans filled with shrapnel and explosives. A short length of fuse with a sulphur top or cap led into the grenade. The munitions were taken into the sorting room at the back of the main office and the pigeonholes were used for segregating the ammunition for the array of weapons that were carried by the Volunteers.

A lorry containing milk cans from the Dairy Engineering Company on Bachelors Walk was commandeered for the purpose of storing water in the event of supplies being shut off. A barricade of bicycles and handcarts was hastily erected to secure the yard.

As Plunkett and Pearse established a command, they were joined by Thomas Clarke and Thomas MacDonagh, who had travelled to the GPO by motorcar. On a table, Plunkett unrolled a map of the city and briefed Captain W. J. Brennan Whitmore on the operation. A number of Cumann na mBán and Fianna Éireann couriers had arrived with despatches from the other commanders in the city.

The 1st Battalion of the Irish Volunteers under Commandant Edward (Ned) Daly had occupied the Four Courts. The 2nd Battalion under Commandant General Thomas MacDonagh had seized Jacob's Biscuit Factory. The 3rd Battalion under Commandant Eamon de Valera had occupied Boland's Mills. The 4th Battalion under Commandant Eamonn Ceannt had taken the South Dublin Union. Units of the Irish Citizen Army under Michael Mallin were in action at St Stephen's Green and also at Dublin Castle.

While the planned explosion of the Magazine Fort in the Phoenix Park that would signal the beginning of the Rising had not been a success, reports were filtering in that many of the insurgents' targets had been secured. The military garrisons in the city, which numbered a little over 2,400 officers and men, had been taken by surprise.

Within the GPO, Pearse ordered Volunteer Michael Staines to take a squad and seize control of the telegraph office, which was located on the second floor. Armed with revolvers, Staines and his men ascended the staircase and were met by a number of hostile staff descending the staircase – although one female employee shouted, 'That's the stuff to give them, Michael.' When the stairs were cleared, the Volunteers were confronted by six British soldiers of the Connaught Rangers who levelled their rifles and ordered the Volunteers to halt. Staines ordered his men to open fire and a British sergeant collapsed as he was hit. The soldiers were quickly disarmed and the sergeant, who had suffered a head wound, was taken to the nearby Jervis Street Hospital for treatment. The soldiers were searched and it was found that they had no ammunition for their weapons. They asked to join the ranks of the Volunteers, but Pearse decided to keep them as prisoners and they were put to work in the field kitchen that was being established by Desmond Fitzgerald. As Staines entered the telegraph office, he found the female supervisor still sending messages. She was ordered to stop but protested, stating that many of the messages were urgent as they contained death notifications. Staines assured her that they would finish the job and she was ushered out the door.[2]

Though a number of phone lines in the city had been cut, the Volunteers had failed to take and secure the Telephone Exchange in Crown Alley. The failure to disable the phone exchange enabled a British adjutant, Colonel Cowan, to place calls through to Portobello, Richmond and the Royal Barracks to advise commanders of the situation that was unfolding in the city and to instruct them to send all troops on 'standby' to secure Dublin Castle, pending a full city mobilisation. At 12.30 hours a telephone message was received at the Curragh Army Camp in County Kildare requesting military assistance in Dublin city. Colonel W. H. M. Lowe, commander of the 3rd Reserve Cavalry Brigade, was briefed on the unfolding situation. A number of calls were also made to Athlone, where the 5th Reserve Artillery Brigade was stationed; to Belfast, where a composite infantry Battalion were mustered; and Templemore, where the 4th Royal Dublin Fusiliers were ordered to mobilise.

At the Curragh Camp, Colonel Lowe ordered a mobile column consisting of the 3rd Reserve Cavalry Brigade to mobilise and immediate entrainment to Kingsbridge Station (now Heuston Station), Dublin, commenced. Grabbing their weapons, twenty-four hours of rations, water and ammunition, the troops made their way to their embarkation point. The British High Command in Ireland issued a *communiqué* via the naval base at Kingstown (now Dún Laoghaire) requesting reinforcements from the War Office in London in order to suppress the armed insurrection.

As the Volunteers in the GPO were preparing to defend it, a number of false alarms were sounded. Shouts of 'here come the military' or 'here's the soldiers' caused a sudden rush to man the barricades and await an attack that never materialised. The Volunteers stood down and resumed their defensive works.[3] A number of shots were accidentally discharged as the Volunteers moved through the building. The sound of breaking glass and the shouts of men reverberated throughout the offices. Sturdy doors that failed to open from a kick were blown open with a revolver shot. Windows were reinforced with sacks, sandbags, boards, typewriters and an array of office paraphernalia. The Volunteers were spread dangerously thin around the building.

Outside, a loud cheer was heard from the crowd as two flags were raised over the General Post Office (I). At the corner of the building, near Henry Street, a tricolour of green, white and orange had been raised on a flagpole. At the Prince's Street corner, a green flag with the words 'Irish Republic' emblazoned upon it was hoisted.

Volunteer Michael Cremen recalled:

> I saw Connolly and Pearse together in the street just as the Tricolour was being hoisted on the GPO. As Connolly shook hands with Pearse, I heard him say, 'Thank God, Pearse, we … have lived to see this day!'[4]

Both officers wondered what the coming hours and days would hold. But it was too late to worry about that now; they were well past the point of no return.

Chapter 3

Easter Monday, 24 April 1916: Afternoon

CONTACT

At 13.00 hours, the Commander-in-Chief of the Army of the Republic and President of the Provisional Government, Patrick Pearse, and Commandant General James Connolly, accompanied by a small escort, made their way out into the portico of the General Post Office. A large crowd of inquisitive onlookers had assembled outside the building. Pearse read out the Proclamation of the Irish Republic to the crowd, who listened to the oration with an air of indifference. The assemblage shuffled around the front of the building, reading the copies of the Proclamation that had been posted up on the walls and pillars of the building.

It was not long before a crowd of 'separation women' had congregated at the entrance to the GPO. The separation women, whose husbands were serving in the British army, feared that their separation payments would not be paid and the crowd soon grew hostile. A number of insults were exchanged between the women and the Volunteers on guard duty.

A line of priests holding hands appeared across Sackville Street and began moving the crowds back towards Carlisle Bridge. As the priests surged forward, individuals broke away and sought refuge in the side streets. Having cleared the people from outside the GPO, they returned up the street to repeat their manoeuvre. However, this time they were met by a hostile mob from the tenements who had no intention of dispersing. The crowd stood firm and then surged forward into the line of priests, breaking their human chain. The priests were soon swallowed up by the throng who ignored their orders to return home. A fatigue party was sent out from the GPO to commandeer food supplies from local shops. Avoiding the mob that had congregated at the front of the building, the armed group moved out and returned laden with supplies, which were deposited in the makeshift kitchen.

An hour after the Irish Republic was established, the first real contact with British armed forces was made. At 12.15 hours the Dublin Metropolitan Police contacted Marlborough Barracks reporting a 'disturbance' in the city and requesting that a cavalry unit be sent to the city centre. Mustering a troop of lancers, Colonel Hammond prepared to carry out a reconnaissance of Sackville Street. The Recce Platoon made their way into the city and stopped briefly at the obelisk commemorating Charles Stewart Parnell. Noticing the large crowd near the GPO, Colonel Hammond ordered his men to move forward in order to investigate. As they trotted off in an even line, the crowd scattered, many dashing into the side streets while the majority moved back towards Carlisle Bridge. The troop cantered down the main street, the pennants of their lances blowing in the gentle spring breeze. Their holstered carbines were testament to the troop's confidence that the sight of the ensemble would be enough to restore order.

Within the GPO the order to 'Stand to' was shouted to the men. Grabbing their weapons, they rushed to the windows and took up firing positions. Connolly stood by one of the lower windows and ordered his men to hold their fire until the Lancers were directly in the firing line. Crouched over their rifles, the men whispered quietly to one another. A short chuckle here, a cough there, the sound of a rifle bolt being pulled back was all that broke the silence.

The Volunteers clicked off the safety catches and squinted over their sights at their assigned frontages. As the horses moved forward, the mounted patrol gathered speed and the canter slowly turned into a gallop. Within thirty yards of the Post Office, despite Connolly's order, a number of shots were fired before a ragged volley was opened up on the patrol. Four troopers fell from their mounts; three dead before they hit the ground, the fourth mortally wounded. Another trooper was thrown from his mount as the animal was cut down in the hail of gunfire. The trooper turned and scrambled for cover towards North Earl Street as rounds whined over his head. A second volley failed to hit any of the remaining patrol who had wheeled their horses around and tried desperately to get out of the line of fire. Colonel Hammond ordered his men to fall back. The Lancers withdrew to the Parnell monument, where they regrouped and remained for a short while before deciding to return to their barracks.[1] In the aftermath of the carnage, an ambulance arrived and conveyed the dead Lancers from the street to the nearby Jervis Street Hospital.

As the action was taking place, Volunteers from the Rathfarnham E Company, who had mobilised late and had made their way to Liberty Hall, were told to report to headquarters at the GPO. Dashing across the broad thoroughfare, the Volunteers reached Prince's Street and attempted to gain access to the building through a side entrance. Finding the door locked, they broke a window and began climbing into the building. As Volunteer John Keely pulled himself onto the windowsill, his gun accidentally discharged, fatally wounding him in the stomach. He was taken to Jervis Street Hospital where he died later that week. John Keely was a fluent Gaelic speaker and he was survived by his wife.

Even though they had suffered one casualty, the mood within the GPO after the Lancers were repulsed was one of jubilation. As the Volunteers ceased firing, reloading clicks of rifle bolts could be heard throughout the building. Within the GPO, Police Constable Edward Dunphy was taken prisoner by Volunteers Joseph Gleeson and John O'Connor (also known as Blimey O'Connor). Other constables on duty in the area hurried back to barracks and reported the situation. Sergeant Michael Soughley wrote:

On the 24th April when the rebellion started we were withdrawn from the streets by order of Colonel E. [Edgeworth] Johnstone, Chief Commissioner, Dublin Metropolitan Police. We had to report to our barracks in the normal way as if reporting for duty during that week. No one interfered with us.[2]

Battleground

The absence of law and order was soon noticed by many citizens, who immediately began taking advantage of the situation. The first victims were sweet and toy shops.

> The plate-glass of Noblett's shivered. The crowd breaks in. A gay shower of sweet-stuffs, chocolate boxes, huge slabs of toffee tosses over amongst the crazy mass. Tyler's suffers in its turn. The old women from the slums literally walk through the plate-glass panes. Heavy fragments of glass crash into their midst inflicting deep gashes and bloody hurts, but their greedy frenzy is unchecked. Purcell's tobacco shop and the Capel Co.'s store are also attacked. Lawrence's net falls a victim. Volunteers emerge and remonstrate, baton and revolver in hand. They deal sturdy blows with rifle butts and threaten with the bayonet's point when all else fails. Rifles are levelled threateningly and once or twice discharged over the looters' heads …[Séan] MacDermott limps across the street and protests vehemently.[3]

The looting spread from Sackville Street into the neighbouring streets. Volunteer Jeremiah O'Leary brought the deteriorating situation to Pearse's notice:

> In the late afternoon, I observed big crowds in Earl Street and Abbey Street, breaking shop windows and beginning to loot the contents…I reported to Pearse and Connolly that disorders were breaking out. Connolly was rather abrupt and probably resentful of my butting in, but Pearse said that there was a shortage of men, that

he had none available to take up police duties, and he asked me to try and organise a Volunteer force to take up the task. He indicated a box of wooden batons which lay in a corner of the main hall and said I might arm the men with these. I went out to the front of the GPO and made a short speech, denouncing the looting and calling for Volunteers to help to suppress it…We moved over towards Earl Street, but there was such a dense, milling crowd there that we became broken up and submerged by the crowd immediately.[4]

Orders were given to Volunteers that looters were to be stopped and if they failed to obey this order they were to be shot. As Helena Moloney was making her way to the GPO, she met Francis Sheehy Skeffington, a known pacifist, who was attempting to organise a civilian police force in order to stop the looting. However, the situation was escalating by the minute:

There was a boot shop at the corner – Tyler's – now Burton's, the tailor's, and the crowd of looters rushed in there and took every pair of boots and shoes in the shop. I actually saw a boy and girl in the office lighting a bundle of papers to set fire to the place. I closed the door and threatened to keep them there unless they put out the fire. They beat it out quickly.[5]

At 16.15 hours the British Quick Reaction Force under the command of Colonel B. P. Portal arrived at Kingsbridge Station. Battalion headquarters were established in the director's office in the train station and soldiers and officers made ready to move out into the city. Intelligence (Intel) reports were filtering in from a variety of sources, identifying a number of insurgent positions around the city. Before any action against could be taken against the insurgents, it was vital for British forces to secure a number of strategic installations and routes into and out of the city. The immediate tasks set by the military were:

a.   To recapture the Magazine Fort in the Phoenix Park.
b.   To secure the Viceregal Lodge.
c.   To relieve and strengthen the military garrison at Dublin Castle.
d.   To obtain reinforcements quickly from at home and from England.

British troops from Portobello, Richmond and the Royal Barracks were ordered to reinforce and secure Dublin Castle. Soldiers from Marlborough Barracks were ordered to secure the Viceregal Lodge and the Magazine Fort and reconnoitre Sackville Street.

Officers waiting in the train station were briefed on the situation and in turn ordered their men to make ready. Weapons were checked and webbing tightened. A company of men was immediately entrained to the North Wall via the loop line, passing under the Phoenix Park, continuing on by the old Cabra Road to Glasnevin, then along the Royal Canal by Cross Guns Bridge, Binns Bridge, Jones Road, Summerhill before finally arriving at the North Wall. Meeting no opposition on their route, they then occupied and secured Amiens Street Train Station (now Connolly Station) and the Custom House.

Units sent from Portobello to Dublin Castle arrived at the complex and immediately took up position. The Royal Dublin Fusiliers had to fight their way through heavy insurgent fire at the Mendicity Institute in order to reach the Castle.

Nearby, the Dublin University Officer Training Corps (OTC) under Captain E. H. Alton and subsequently G. A. Harris managed to secure Trinity College and fortify the complex against a possible attack. Eight men had managed to close the main gates and secure the building. They then set about increasing their ranks by offering refuge to soldiers who were on leave or who found themselves cut off from their depots. Arms were procured from the OTC armoury and distributed to the makeshift garrison. Having secured all entry and exit points, the soldiers and members of the OTC took up positions on the upper floors of the college. Fields of fire covered the surrounding streets, but more importantly severed the Volunteer communication lines between the Volunteer garrisons at St Stephen's Green and the General Post Office (I).

By late afternoon, British troops were advancing into the city through the northern suburbs. Major Somerville, commander of the School of Musketry at Dollymount, had led a company of soldiers into the city and had managed to secure the North Wall Railway Station. He ordered his men to press forward and use the railway line to guide them towards Amiens Street Station. They were challenged, however, by Volunteer Captain Tom Weafer's 2nd Battalion, who with one hundred men held Clarke's Bridge over the Royal Canal. A fierce gun battle erupted between the opposing forces. Captain Weafer was escorting a convoy of vital military supplies to the GPO when his unit made 'contact'. He immediately divided his force into three:

Section One was ordered to fight a rearguard action at the bridge, Section Two was ordered to seize defensive positions at Ballybough Bridge and control road and rail approaches, Section Three was to continue with the convoy to the GPO. The Volunteer rearguard took up position commanding Annesley Railway Bridge. Defensive posts were established in the corner houses in North Strand, Annesley Place, Spring Garden Street and Leinster Avenue. The military pushed forward towards the bridge and were immediately engaged by the Volunteers. There were sharp cracks of rifle fire, which forced the British troops to take cover. The British soldiers tried to bring a machine gun to bear on the Irish positions, but the Volunteers returned fire and eliminated the threat. The soldiers retreated, scrambling over the open ground as bullets kicked up the dirt around them. Realising that the insurgents were ensconced in their positions, the military decided to get out of the kill zone and made their way off the railway line and into the side streets. Realising that the British attack had stalled, Captain Weafer took advantage of the situation and withdrew his men to the GPO where they arrived safely later that afternoon.

Captain Weafer reported to Commandant Connolly and submitted a situation report. He was ordered to 'stand by' and await further orders. After the briefing, Connolly and Plunkett knew that the British had commenced their advance on the city and it would only be a matter of time before an all-out attack was launched on the Volunteers' GHQ. The hourglass was quickly running out.

Chapter 4

Easter Monday, 24 April 1916: Defensive Posts

As the GPO was being occupied, a defensive perimeter was being established around the building and the surrounding area. The positioning of these defensive fighting posts in the immediate vicinity of GHQ commanded the routes that the British army could use to attack. Due to the lack of manpower, however, many of these posts were undermanned.

The Volunteers that had secured Carlisle Bridge were ordered to occupy two positions that commanded the approach to the bridge: the jewellers Hopkins and Hopkins (U) on Eden Quay and Kelly's Gunpowder Store, later to become known as 'Kelly's Fort' (V) on Bachelors Walk. Volunteer Peadar Bracken took a squad and occupied Kelly's while Seamus Robinson took two men and broke into Hopkins and Hopkins. Both posts provided a commanding field of fire over the bridge and the quays. On entering the buildings, the Volunteers began barricading the entrances and fortifying the windows. Both units began tunnelling or mouse-holing back through the buildings towards Abbey Street. By interconnecting the buildings, the Volunteers could move without exposing themselves to enemy fire. While many of the Volunteers were armed with shotguns, one Volunteer stationed in Kelly's had a Belgian-made automatic rifle.[1] Though the ammunition for this weapon was limited, it could fire its five-round magazine on automatic.

Frank Thornton's company, which had failed to occupy the Telephone Exchange, withdrew under fire from the area and occupied buildings on Fleet Street. They sent a despatch to GHQ informing them of their position. Commandant General Connolly ordered them to hold their position for a possible attack on Trinity College. This plan was abandoned, however, and Thornton's unit were ordered to return to GHQ.[2] As they arrived, they were ordered to occupy and secure Clery's/Imperial Hotel (J) on Sackville Street. Moving at the double, the group, composed of Citizen Army and 2nd Battalion Volunteers, crossed the street and took control of the hotel.

At the GPO, Commandant General Connolly formed a group at the front of the building. Dividing the group into three, he instructed Frank Henderson to take the first twenty men and occupy positions in Henry Street; Leo Henderson was to take another twenty men and reinforce the garrison at the Clery's/Imperial Hotel (J) Block. The remaining men, under the command of Oscar Traynor, were ordered to occupy the block of buildings from Prince's Street to Abbey Street, which included the Metropole Hotel (M), Eason's (N) and Manfield's boot store. On entering the hotel, Lieutenant Traynor explained the purpose of their mission to the manger as his men began turning the guests out of their rooms. Hotel windows were smashed and barricades of furniture were erected over the sills. That night, the Volunteers tunnelled from the drawing room of the Hotel Metropole (M) through to the first floor of Eason's (N) and then continued into Manfield's. From the quays, the Volunteers could utilise the warren of streets and alleys and move with ease from one post to another.

To cover the rear of the GPO, squads were deployed into Liffey Street and Middle Abbey Street, where a barricade was constructed. The old Independent building and Lucas' Cycle Shop were occupied by Volunteers who immediately began barricading the doors and windows. Number 1A Liffey Street was occupied by a squad who took up firing positions on the upper floors. These posts covered the approaches from Capel Street.

Another squad occupied the Coliseum Theatre (G) on Henry Street and put the building in a state of defence. Volunteer Michael Knightly took up sentry duty at the door of the theatre.

The upper storeys of houses ('The Arch') on Henry Street were secured by a squad which barricaded the entrances and took up firing positions at the windows. The rest of Henry Street was secured by squads that occupied MacInerney and Co., Bewley Sons and Co., and Arnott and Co. Ltd. Drapers (E). Each building was put in a state of defence and the Volunteers took up their firing positions.

Connolly believed that the British would launch an infantry attack up Lower Abbey Street from Amiens Street Railway Station. Captain W. J. Brennan Whitmore was ordered to 'take and hold' positions on North Earl Street. His orders read:

Battleground

A report has just come in that the British have occupied Amiens Street Station in force. We anticipate an assault on our headquarters at any moment. You will take these men, occupy North Earl Street, break in and fortify the block down as far as the Imperial Hotel. As there is no post between the enemy and our headquarters you will defend this position to the last man.[3]

Whitmore assembled his unit and moved out across Sackville Street towards Noblett's corner. The Volunteers entered the building, which housed Noblett's Sweet Shop (A) and the Pillar Café (A).

As the entrance was secured, the task of barricading the windows began. In order to stop any advance by the enemy, Captain Whitmore began the construction of a barricade across North Earl Street. Furniture was thrown from the windows and piled high across the street. Looters arrived on the scene and attempted to take the furniture from the obstruction. Whitmore drew his automatic pistol and ordered the items to be returned. The barricade was reinforced and secured by winding a coil of copper wire through the items and securing each end to the poles and lamp standards on each side of the street. A number of reinforcements arrived at the post and Whitmore put them to work loop-holing the walls to make firing positions. A scout was sent towards Amiens Street Station to verify the report that British troops were in possession of the building. He returned later and reported that the station seemed to be unoccupied – this gave Whitmore more time to fortify his position.

Whitmore established contact with Frank Thornton's unit, which had occupied the adjacent Clery's/Imperial Hotel (J). The property of William Martin Murphy, the prime antagonist during the 1913 Lockout, the hotel was carefully chosen as the fields of fire from the building covered a number of approaches to the area. Volunteer Frank Thornton and his unit had unfurled the Citizen Army flag, the Starry Plough, over the building. The task of linking the hotel with Captain Whitmore's post began in earnest and each group began mouse-holing through the block. Captain Whitmore designated the Imperial Hotel as a command post (CP).

The Volunteers began clearing the area of civilians and a number of occupied shops were emptied at gunpoint. Whitmore entered Fagan's public house and climbed out onto the roof where the owner, an old Fenian, identified the principal buildings and main approaches to the operational area. Within a few hours, Whitmore had secured the area and, having completed his mission, telephoned the GPO and reported that the block was secure and that all was quiet.

Joseph Plunkett ordered Volunteer Fergus O'Kelly to take a squad and seize the Dublin Wireless School of Telegraphy, which was located on the top floor of a building known as Reis's and Co. (R) on the corner of the block between Lower Abbey Street and the River Liffey. In order for the insurrection to be a success, the world would have to be informed that an independent Irish Republic had been declared and the best way to achieve this was by wireless. The building had been closed by the authorities at the beginning of the First World War and most of the transmitting apparatus had been dismantled. Taking his squad, which consisted of David Bourke, Arthur

Shields and John O'Connor (known as 'Blimey'), the group crossed Sackville Street and forced entry into the building. While some of the men began securing the post, Bourke began to reassemble the apparatus. O'Kelly discovered that the aerial on the roof had been taken down but the two poles were still present. He ordered that the poles be re-erected and sent a Volunteer to scour the surrounding shops for suitable electrical wire. Realising his post could be exposed to enemy fire, he reported the fact to Connolly at GHQ.

In response to this information, Commandant Connolly despatched Captain Thomas Weafer with a company to block access to Sackville Street by barricading Lower Abbey Street, thus ensuring the security of the entire block. In order to build the barricade, Weafer commandeered several large reels of newsprint from an *Irish Times* warehouse. The obstruction was reinforced with thousands of pounds worth of motorcycles taken from a local shop that were piled up against the paper barricade. Weafer and his unit then took up position within the Hibernian Bank (Q).

On the roof of Reis's (R), the aerial was erected but in order to get the transmitter working, Blimey O'Connor was detailed to climb the wireless mast and repair the wiring. As he was carrying out the work, sniper fire erupted from across the river. Bullets whistled through the air as a British marksman tried to hit his target. O'Connor managed to avoid being shot and the job was completed in double-quick time – the plan had worked. Though the transmitter could send out messages, the receiver failed to work. The message, 'Irish Republic declared in Dublin today, Irish troops have captured the city and are in full possession. Enemy cannot move in city. The whole country is Rising' was tapped out continuously for hours. Ships at sea picked up the message and relayed it to America and the continent.

Nearby, the Dublin Bread Company (DBC) (T), a well-known restaurant, was occupied by a squad and subsequently reinforced by a section sent by Captain Weafer. This observation post (OP) gave an eagles-eye view of the city. The Volunteers began mouse-holing from building to building and within hours the block had been linked. Towards evening, Captain Whitmore divided his command into sections, detailing the least fatigued men for 'first watch'. As Whitmore made his way onto the roof of their command post (CP), he ordered his second in command, Lieutenant Gerald Crofts, to arrange breakfast for the men for early in the morning.

Though the Volunteers were unable to secure the whole area, they had managed to occupy a number of strategic posts that covered most of the approaches to the GPO. Believing that the British would launch an assault on their position from the east, Connolly and Plunkett had left the area to the north of the GPO devoid of any outposts. This was to prove detrimental to their plan.

Chapter 5

Easter Monday,
24 April 1916: Evening

By 18.00 hours, six hours into the operation, the Volunteers had secured their GHQ and most of the surrounding area.

Throughout the day there had been a steady stream of Volunteers making their way to the GPO, having heard that the Rising was in progress. At the General Post Office, J. J. Walsh arrived with thirty members of the Hibernian Rifles. A unit of Volunteers from Maynooth led by Captain Tom Byrne also arrived at the building with both officers reporting to republican command at the GPO. Commandant Connolly sent both units to reinforce the garrison at City Hall but they were unable to break through and instead occupied the Exchange Hotel in Parliament Street. After beating off repeated enemy assaults they were called back to GHQ and stationed throughout the building. There was an international flavour to the garrison when two foreign sailors arrived at the Post Office and offered their services. When questioned by Volunteer Liam Tannam as to why they wanted to fight, the sailors replied:

The smaller of the two spoke. He said, 'I am from Sweden, my friend from Finland. We want to fight. May we come in?' I asked him why a Swede and a Finn would want to fight against British rule. He said, 'Finland, a small country, Russia eat her up'. Then he said: 'Sweden, another small country, Russia eat her up too. Russia with the British, therefore, we against.'[1]

Winifred Carney had set up office with her typewriter near the central command point in the building. Connolly dictated a number of orders that were typed and prepared for despatch.

A throng of young women and boys concealed the messages under their hats or had them sewn into the lining of their clothes before being sent out to the various Volunteer posts throughout the city.

Áine Heron was ordered to report to the Hibernian Bank (Q) on Abbey Street. She recalled:

When we emerged from the G.P.O. I felt scared for the first time. There was a crowd of drunken women who had been looting public houses and other shops. They had their arms full of the loot. They were at the other side of the road and they called out all sorts of names at us, but they were too drunk to attack us.[2]

One of the first buildings to catch fire was the Cable Shoe Shop. A Dublin Fire Brigade tender under Captain Purcell arrived on the scene and the firemen set about rescuing a number of people from the upper floors and bringing the fire under control. As they were fighting the conflagration, the looters set fire to another building and Captain Purcell was forced to call for more support to control the fires.

Within the GPO, Volunteers James Ryan and Dan McLoughlin, both medical students, were ordered to report to the improvised field hospital, which had been set up at the rear of the GPO, assisted by a section of the Cumann na mBán. The initial casualties suffered from superficial injuries such as cuts and bruises which had occurred while fortifying the building.

Fr John O'Flanagan was brought to the GPO where he listened to confessions and aided the wounded. He was asked to remain at his post and was to become the garrison priest for the remainder of the week.

Outside, the looting and destruction of property continued throughout the day and into the evening:

> I remember we were still on the roof when Lawrence's
> (C) went on fire. It was a sports shop, and all the kids
> brought out a lot of fireworks, made a huge pile of them
> in the middle of O'Connell Street and set fire to them.
> That is one thing that will stick in my mind forever. We
> had our bombs on top of the Post Office, and these
> fireworks were shooting up in the sky. We were very ner-
> vous. There were Catherine wheels going up O'Connell
> Street and Catherine wheels coming down O'Connell
> Street.[3]

As Volunteer Lieutenant Liam Clarke unloaded a number of homemade bombs from a handcart, one of them exploded, causing him severe facial injuries. He was evacuated from the building and taken to Jervis Street Hospital. Realising that the bombs were unstable, a group of Volunteers took a number of them outside and placed them at the bottom of Nelson's Pillar in order to test them. Explosions rocked the base of the monument, proving that the bombs, though dangerous, were viable improvised explosive devices.

Volunteers Jack Plunkett, Joseph Reilly and Ernest and John Nunan began tunnelling at the back of the GPO in order to provide a line of retreat if the building were to be stormed by the enemy.

Though reports were filtering in of progress in Dublin, very little was coming from the rest of the country. Many intelligence reports were inaccurate and often fabricated. Rumours abounded as to what was happening not only in Dublin but throughout the country:

> Some said the Germans had landed here, there and everywhere – a German submarine was coming up the Liffey – the Volunteers were marching in from the coun-try – the whole of the country was up in arms…The German fleet was in the Bay![4]

Most units seemed to have been stood down, leaving the Dublin battalions on their own.

As the GPO garrison settled down for the evening, many of them busied themselves with the tasks of cleaning and maintaining their weapons. Sentries were posted throughout the building. The officers sat together reading through the situation reports that had filtered into headquarters throughout the day. The Rising was going according to plan even though the turnout was poor. The Volunteers sank down where they could and tried to make themselves comfortable for the night. Morale was high and the next day held much hope for them.

The displaced GPO staff had established a vital communications (comms) link from Amiens Street Station, which linked Dublin and London with a direct line between the Government's Irish office and its counterpart in London. As there was no direct link between the Castle and Amiens Street, telegraph engineers routed a line through Crown Alley exchange, which had not been disabled by the insurgents. An engineer travelled around the city, restoring communications and rerouting lines via private circuits. This enabled the British army to communicate with their posts around the city.

At 18.11 hours, Sir Matthew Nathan, the Under Secretary in the Irish Office and the most senior civil servant in Ireland, sent the following Situation Report (Sitrep) from Dublin Castle to Augustine Birrell in London:

Insurrection broke out noon today in Dublin when attack made on castle but not pressed home. Since then large hostile parties have occupied Stephen's Green, and various parties have held up troops marching from barracks firing on them from houses. City Hall, Post Office, Four Courts, Westland Row Station occupied by Sinn Féiners, some railway bridges blown up and telegraph communication completely interrupted. Have information two policemen, one military officer and half dozen soldiers killed but casualties may be much more numerous.

> Situation at present not satisfactory but understand troops now beginning to arrive from Curragh.[5]

As the Sitrep was sent, the 59th North Midland Division under the command of Major-General A. E. Sandbach, CB, DSO, received orders from Brigade HQ to 'stand to' for an immediate move. The division, located in England, consisted of three brigades: 176th (2/5th, 2/6th South Staffordshire Regiment, 2/5th, 2/6th North Staffordshire Regiment); 177th (2/4th, 2/5th Lincolnshire Regiment, 2/4th, 2/5th Leicestershire Regiment) and the 178th infantry division (2/5th, 2/6th, 2/7th and 2/8th Battalions of the Sherwood Forester Regiment).[6]

Many men had obtained leave for the holiday weekend and as they returned to barracks they were informed of the impending move. Soldiers from each battalion were furnished with forty-eight hours' dry rations and a quantity of ammunition. Morale amongst the rank and file was high as it was expected that the Division was on the move to the Western Front. Within twenty-four hours, however, thousands of British soldiers would be reinforcing Dublin city's garrisons and the battle would begin in earnest.

Chapter 6

Tuesday, 25 April 1916:
FOB Trinity

At 00.30 hours, three cyclists peddled down Grafton Street, heading towards the GPO. Headed by Volunteer Gerald Keogh, the three cyclists had been despatched to Larkfield by Commandant Pearse to secure arms and ammunition and were on the return journey. They had passed their colleagues at St Stephens's Green and were nearing College Green. Each man carried two rifles, one of which was attached to the bicycle, the other being slung over their shoulders. The ammunition, consisting of over 400 rounds, was carried in haversacks secured on their backs. A volley of shots rang out from Trinity College, killing Gerald Keogh instantly. His companions were wounded but managed to get out of the line of fire and double back towards the Green where they reported the incident. Gerald Keogh was twenty years old and was an apprentice in the drapery trade. His death left a widowed mother and three young siblings.

With the help of three men, acting porter George Crawford retrieved the body and brought it into the Provost's house.

The shots had been fired by members of the Australia and New Zealand Army Corps (ANZACS), who were positioned at the upper windows of the college. An unnamed student who used the pseudonym 'One of the Garrison' described the shooting:

> The ANZACS had been above on the roof of the college since an early hour. Owing to the strict order received from the Irish Command not to fire until attacked, many chances of 'potting' rebels had been missed. But later in the morning this order had been withdrawn. Already before daylight a despatch rider of the enemy had been brought down by the fire of the ANZACS. It was wonderful shooting. He was one of three who were riding past on bicycles. Four shots were fired. Three found their mark in the head of the unfortunate victim. Another of the riders was wounded and escaped on foot. The third abandoned his bicycle and also escaped. This shooting was done by uncertain light of the electric lamps, at a high angle downwards from a lofty building. The body was brought in.
>
> Later I saw him. In no irreverent spirit I lifted the face-cloth. He looked quite young; one might almost call him a boy. The handsome waxen face was on one side concealed in blood.[1]

For three days the body lay in an empty room in the college before it was taken outside and interred in a makeshift grave in the grounds of the college. A letter from eyewitness Gerard Fitzgibbon to William Hugh Blake in May 1916 states:

We planted him out later on to fertilise the Provost's daf-fodils.[2]

A number of colonial soldiers from South Africa, New Zealand, Canada and Australia were stationed within the college, having been secreted into the complex by a number of students.

The unnamed 'One of the Garrison' wrote:

Stray soldiers were summoned from the adjacent streets and from the Central Soldiers' Club hard by the college to reinforce the garrison; these included some 'ANZAC' sharpshooters.[3]

James Glen, a British soldier, was strolling down O'Connell Street with a friend when shots were fired at them. He wrote:

We realized that we were probably the target and ran down to O'Connell Bridge where we were joined by about a dozen soldiers (Australians, and I think one or two South Africans) who were on leave and had been attracted by the firing. My friend and I ... took the party into [the] college ... the Australians and South Africans volunteered to man the roof overlooking College Green, where there were the best opportunities for experienced riflemen.[4]

Some of these men had been on furlough or on sick leave from the front when they were caught up in events. At 04.00 hours Brigadier General Lowe, Commanding the 3rd Reserve Cavalry Brigade (in the absence since the Friday of the

Commander-in-Chief, Ireland, Major General L. B. Friend), arrived in Kingsbridge Station from the Curragh. Accompanying him were 1,000 troops of the 25th Irish Infantry Brigade. His mission was to retake and hold Dublin city. Establishing a Tactical Operations Centre (TOC) within Kingsbridge Station, Lowe immediately set about his first task, which was to relieve and secure Dublin Castle. There had been intelligence reports of heavy insurgent activity in Sackville Street and around the Four Courts on the quays. Lowe gathered his officers and senior NCOs together for an 'orders group' and relayed his plans to retake the city. Colonel Portal was ordered to establish a line of posts from Kingsbridge Station to Trinity College via Dublin Castle and Dame Street. This course of action would divide the positions of the Irish Volunteers north and south of the River Liffey, enabling Crown forces to establish a safe line of advance and communication.

By early morning reports were filtering back to Lowe that the insurgents who had occupied City Hall and Dame Street had either been killed or captured and that the area of operations had been secured. At St Stephen's Green rebel forces had been forced out of the park and were holed up within the College of Surgeons. Further information revealed that the two main insurgent positions were located at the Four Courts and the General Post Office (I) in Sackville Street.

Trinity College was being held by 150 soldiers and OTC, whose occupation of the college had driven a wedge between insurgent positions. Utilising the college as a Forward Operations Base (FOB), General Lowe's troops could use the buildings as a staging area to launch an attack on the rebel headquarters at the GPO.

Dublin Castle could also be used as a staging area, making these two British positions vital posts for retaking the city. Lowe would then launch a coordinated attack as soon as his men were in position and within range.

In Trinity College, the snipers in the upper storeys aligned the sights of their weapons and zeroed in on Sackville Street. Looking out onto the streets below, the soldiers spied the distinctive, self-contained and troublesome rectangle of Sackville Street with its narrow side streets and alleyways flanked by enemy defensive posts, which they knew were an insurgent's paradise. Spotters scanned the streetscape locating Volunteer posts for the marksmen. Since the order not to engage had been lifted, Sackville Street had become a free-fire zone and any person in the vicinity could be considered a combatant. As the spring day dawned, the soldiers picked the best line of fire, determining the wind direction and adjusting their sights to compensate.

The snipers set the brassbacked wooden butts of their Lee Enfield rifles against their shoulders, placed their cheeks next to the rear sights, squinted down the barrels, released their breaths to steady their torsos and began squeezing off shots. Bolts were drawn back and spent cartridges were ejected from the weapons; the new rounds were pushed into place as the bolts closed, ready for the next shot. 'One of the Garrison' wrote:

> After being relieved, I joined the ANZACS on the roof. They were undoubtedly men fashioned for the enjoyment of danger. And certainly it would be harder to find nicer comrades. Alas, for thousands of these fine soldiers who have left their bones on Gallipoli![5]

The British managed to insert a sniper into McBirney's, a large department store located on Aston Quay, south of the River Liffey. Taking up his position on the upper middle floor, the sniper opened fire on the Volunteers in Kelly's Fort (V) and Hopkins and Hopkins(U). Bullets smashed into the buildings, splintering the woodwork and sending up clouds of plaster dust. Both garrisons could make out the zip-zip noise of incoming rounds.

Pinned down and unable to return fire because of their inadequate weapons, the Volunteers tried desperately to cast eyes on whoever was attacking their posts. Using the network of mouse-holes, the Volunteers were able to get to the GPO, pick up more adequate weapons and ammunition and return to Kelly's Fort (V) without exposing themselves to enemy fire. Having emptied a number of magazines into both Volunteer posts, the sniper began working on opportunity. He began selecting random targets from the civilian population and, taking deliberate aim, opened fire, hitting a number of men and women before turning his attention to a blind man traversing the street. As the bullet struck and the man collapsed motionless to the ground, a member of the St John's Ambulance ran to administer first aid to the victim. A second shot rang out, hitting the good Samaritan and sending him crashing to the ground. Both wounded men struggled to their feet and staggered out of the line of fire to the relative safety of Westmorland Street.

The Volunteers knew that they had only one chance to find and take out the Mark (enemy sniper) before he realised his hide was compromised, thus forcing him to move position. Volunteer Cormac Turner, stationed in Hopkins and Hopkins, had procured a pair of binoculars and scanned the surrounding buildings for the enemy marksman. Turner identified one of the top windows of McBirney's as the sniper's position and noted that the gunman was using a number of the employees who were watching from the windows to cover his activities. Having pinpointed the enemy post, Turner relayed the information across the street to those in Kelly's Fort (V), coordinating a plan to neutralise the threat. Turner watched the window of McBirney's through his binoculars and directed Volunteer Andrew Conroy to take up a firing position at the window of Hopkins and Hopkins. Conroy swung his .303 rifle up into his shoulder, took careful aim and waited for the order to fire. As the enemy sniper reappeared at the window and prepared to shoot, Turner shouted 'Fire.' A volley of shots rang out from both Volunteer posts. As Turner watched through the binoculars, he witnessed the enemy gunman spin and fall backwards as the bullets hit their target. Though one position had been taken out, those marksmen on the roof of Trinity College had been reinforced. A Lewis machine gun was set up on the rooftop of the college and zeroed in on Hopkins and Hopkins and Kelly's Fort (V). The gunner checked his magazine, took aim and opened fire. Rounds slammed into the buildings, shattering the remainder of the glass and sending up plumes of red brick dust into the air. The Volunteers dived for cover as the relentless chatter of machine gun fire reverberated throughout the building and into the streets below.

Chapter 7

Tuesday, 25 April 1916:
Hold and Secure

Within the General Post Office (I), the chaotic scenes of the previous day's occupation were slowly giving way to some order:

Upstairs on the top story of the building the [G.]P.O. restaurant has been turned into a Volunteer mess-quarters. Desmond Fitzgerald, at the head of a busy ration party, is preparing breakfast for the few hundred defenders of the G.P.O. Five or six Tommies have also been requisitioned. By this time everyone has been allotted to his different station and the building no longer presents the appearance of an overturned anthill, as was the case the evening before. All street-facing windows have been barricaded and manned by single, double or treble guards of Volunteers, as the case may have demanded. An ambulance department and hospital have been prepared. Armourers have collected all the loose and spare ammunition, rifles, revolvers, pikes etc., into one central depot. Another room has been set apart for hand and fuse grenades. Chemical fire extinguishers are distributed at the different danger points, while in the yard outside other parties are busy filling sandbags.[1]

Exhaustion consumed the leaders:

> Behind the central counter mattresses had been placed. Here, Pearse, Connolly, Plunkett, MacDermott and Tom Clarke slept in turns. They all had to be given opium, according to a Red Cross worker, before they could sleep. Beds were brought in later for them. On the Tuesday morning they were all seated together on boxes and barrels, pale and tired. But they were very calm and humorous…MacDermott was as gentle and as fiery as he always was. Tom Clarke seemed quite at home.[2]

The leaders of the insurrection assembled in one of the rooms for a morning briefing.

Volunteer Charles J. MacAuley wrote:

> In a tiny room there was a group of people whom I remember very distinctly. Stretched on a pallet on the floor was Joseph Plunkett in riding breeches and wearing a green Volunteer uniform shirt. In the room also seated there was Tom Clarke in civilian clothes with a bandolier across his shoulders and a rifle between his knees. He was silent and had a look of grim determination on his face. I was greatly impressed by him. It was as if he thought his day had come. He never spoke … The last thing I

remember about the Post Office in the early hours of Easter Tuesday morning was being escorted to the top of the stairs leading down to the ground floor by Seán MacDermott. He shook hands with me at the top of the stairs. He had a charming personality and appeared calm and gracious as usual. But I felt an element of sadness in his farewell.[3]

Holding the rank of Commandant General of the Dublin Division, James Connolly directed the military aspects of the insurrection while Pearse, as President of the Republic, impressed the men with his inspiring rhetoric. Oscar Traynor recalled:

Pearse assured the men that they had done a great and noble work for their country, and said that if they did not do anything else they had at least redeemed the fair name of Dublin city, which was dishonoured when [Robert] Emmet was allowed to die before a large crowd of its people. He said: 'Be assured that you will find victory, even though that victory may be found in death'. That was another terribly thrilling moment.[4]

Connolly and Pearse both toured the posts, inspecting their men and assuring them all was going well. Connolly issued the following order to the officer in charge of Reis's (R) and the DBC (T):

The main purpose of your post is to protect our wireless station. Its secondary purpose is to observe Lower Abbey Street and Lower O'Connell Street.

Commandeer in the D.B.C. whatever food and utensils you require. Make sure of a plentiful supply of water wherever your men are. Break all glass in the windows of the rooms occupied by you for fighting purposes. Establish a connection between your forces in the D.B.C. and Reis's building. Be sure that the stairways leading immediately to your rooms are well barricaded.

We have a post in the corner of Bachelors Walk, in the Metropole Hotel, in the Imperial Hotel, in the General Post Office. The directions from which you are likely to be attacked are from the Custom House and from the far side of the river, D'Olier Street or Westmorland Street. We believe there is a sniper in McBirneys on the far side of the river.[5]

Defences were checked and commented upon before both officers returned to GHQ. By 12.00 hours the Volunteers had secured all the buildings from Lower Abbey Street to Sackville Place and from the corner of Eden Quay up to North Earl Street. Every building on both sides of Lower Sackville Street could be traversed through a series of holes that had been bored from building to building. Connolly toured the positions inspecting barricades and, as reinforcements arrived, positions were strengthened and lines extended. Barbed wire was rolled out at the front of the GPO in case of a frontal assault by the British. Tram lines were taken down and used to reinforce barricades.

In order to alert Volunteer command to any possible attack a communications system was established by Volunteers William Daly and Joe Good. They ran a phone line from the roof to the ground floor and so the approach of the enemy from any direction could be reported immediately to GHQ command.

The Volunteers were ordered to search the GPO for arms and ammunition. A number of safes were forced open and found to contain only money, which was then secured. Volunteers Joseph Duffy and Patrick Colgan began searching the office of the Secretary of the General Post Office. Colgan wrote:

> Duffy and I continued to force open presses, desks and boxes in the room. In one press we found the blood-stained 2/lieutenant's British army uniform of a son of the secretary. He had been killed in France some short time earlier. In an envelope we found a lock of his fair hair, marked by the boy's mother. I forgot the name of the boy. With the uniform was a .45 revolver in a holster. Duffy having reported the finding of the revolver was allowed to retain it.[6]

Outside in the streets, the looting was continuing. Volunteer Thomas Leahy wrote:

> The whole populace was very much dumbfounded and their long suffering under the economic conditions and low wages for their labour made them more determined to grab all they could. It was a pity to see them, especially able-bodied men doing this kind of thing, instead of being in the firing line with us.[7]

The Volunteers were powerless to deal with the escalating situation and any attempt to try and stop the hordes of looters was defeated due to the lack of manpower.

Battleground

In order to get a foothold on Sackville Street, a fire-team of British soldiers moved at the double down the street and rushed the Gresham Hotel. Guests were ordered to the rear of the building as the military barricaded the entrance and took up positions on the upper floors overlooking the street below. A gun battle erupted between the Gresham Hotel and the insurgents on the roof of the GPO. The sound of shattering glass and splintering wood echoed throughout the street. Volunteer James Kelly was shot dead with a bullet to the head. He was fifteen years old and a fitter's apprentice.

On the south side of the river, a machine-gun unit moved out from Trinity and set up a post in Purcell's shop on the corner of Westmorland and D'Olier Street. Automatic fire was directed against the insurgent posts on the quays.

Volunteer forces sabotaged the rail line near Fairview Park close to the East Wall Road, forcing the composite battalion from Belfast to detrain. They began to move towards the city via the Drumcondra Road. A battery of four 18-pounders of the Royal Artillery under Major G. N. Hill was entrained from Athlone. On reaching Blanchardstown, the battery was detrained and moved by road to Phibsborough.

Volunteer Michael Knightly made his way to the GPO and was debriefed by Seán MacDermott:

Seán MacDermott came to the door, shook hands and introduced me to The O'Rahilly. 'Have you got any news?' he asked eagerly. 'The only news I have,' I replied, 'is that artillery are on their way from Athlone.' 'Damn it,' he said, 'only for MacNeill yesterday we would have had the whole country with us. As it is we might get some terms.' To this I did not reply. I had heard the matter discussed by my colleagues during the day and one conclusion came to was that every man who signed the Proclamation would be shot.[8]

Connolly and Plunkett realised that a nationwide revolt had not materialised. The plan to trap the British between republican forces in the cities and those from the country had failed. Connolly began to devise a new strategy, one of a siege, in the hope that Volunteer forces throughout the country would rise and relieve the city garrison before they were forced to capitulate. His disposition of Volunteers would force the British into an all-out frontal assault on their positions. Connolly believed that the enemy would commit infantry rather than artillery to the battle as the British would not destroy Dublin city. The fighting he envisaged would end in hand-to-hand combat, a fight to the bitter end. Forty-eight hours of the new Republic had been devoted to preparation, occupation and fortification of their posts.

On entering the outskirts of the north of the city, British forces were immediately faced by enemy contact. The artillery was brought into action to remove barricades at the Cabra and North Circular Road Bridges. The fire fight was brief but intense and the Volunteers were ordered to disengage and pull out. This permitted the 4th Royal Dublin Fusiliers to move forward and secure Glasnevin and the Finglas Road. With these roads closed down, the Volunteer's escape route through the northern suburbs had been severed, and the military were moving ever deeper into the city of Dublin.

Chapter 8

Wednesday, 26 April 1916: No Man's Land

By 00.00 hours Sackville Street had become a ghostly no man's land. Debris from the previous day's lootings lay scattered across the street. The rotting corpse of the Lancer's horse and the abandoned tram had become a grotesque part of the streetscape.

At 00.20 hours, scouts reported to GHQ that overwhelming enemy forces were encircling the city. Commandant Connolly ordered the platoon of Volunteers that had controlled the suburb at Fairview and had held Annesley Bridge since noon on Monday to fall back and reinforce headquarters. The platoon pulled out, taking with them some British soldiers they had taken prisoner, including Captain George Mahony of the Indian Medical Service who had been captured near Drumcondra. The unit reached Sackville Street without encountering enemy forces and rushed out from Sackville Place in extended order towards the GPO. Those on sentry duty, believing that the building was being stormed by the British, opened fire. Volunteer Billy

McGinly was wounded in the 'blue on blue' situation (opening fire on your own side) before Commandant Connolly ordered his men to cease fire. The khaki uniforms of the prisoners had given the sentries the impression that an attack was being launched. On entering the Post Office, the Volunteers reported on the worsening situation in the city to Commandant Connolly. After a brief respite the men were deployed to reinforce the garrison in the nearby Metropole Hotel (M). The prisoners were put to work in the mess hall while Captain George Mahony was escorted to the Volunteers' makeshift hospital and began assisting with the wounded.

The sentries posted within the GPO looked out over the deserted Dublin streets. As the garrison within the GPO was beginning to wake, General Lowe put his plan to retake Dublin city into effect.

Lowe's strategy consisted of erecting a cordon around the city and then a smaller cordon around the enemy's main positions that were identified as being their GHQ in Sackville Street and the Four Courts. The first of the smaller cordons would run from Dublin Castle, down Dame Street to Trinity College, across Butt Bridge to the Custom House to link up with Amiens Street Station. The cordon would continue up Gardiner Street into Lower Britain Street, across the top of O'Connell Street at the Parnell monument and over into Capel Street. It would then move back down across the river and back to the Castle. This would drive a wedge between the two main Volunteer positions. Secure in the knowledge that a British Division had landed in Kingstown and would be soon making their way into the city, General Lowe decided to bypass the outer ring of rebel posts. However, two obstacles would have to be removed in order to enable the British to erect a cordon around the city: Liberty Hall and the Mendicity Institute. General Lowe had reinforced the garrison within Trinity with a company of soldiers from the Leinster Regiment and an artillery piece from Athlone. Machine guns had been mounted at vantage points in and around the college. A number of troops had also occupied the Custom House and were preparing to storm across Beresford Place and take Liberty Hall. Unknown to the attackers, Liberty Hall was empty.

At 08.00 hours the gunboat HMS *Helga* sailed up the River Liffey and took up a firing position outside the Custom House. Pressed into service at the outbreak of the First World War as an armed auxiliary patrol yacht, the former Department of Agriculture ship had been fitted out with a quick firing 12-pound gun aft and a smaller 3-pound 'pom pom' to the stern. The front gun, with a range of 11,000 metres and a firing rate of fifteen rounds per minute, was manned by two sailors who loaded a shell into the gun's breech and aimed the weapon at Liberty Hall. As the gun fired, the shell hit the metal railway bridge with a resounding clang that echoed throughout the city. Reloading the weapon, the sailors realigned the gun and fired. A foot-long flame stabbed from the gun's muzzle as the weapon recoiled. There was a near simultaneous flash and a thunderous crump as the shell detonated and Liberty Hall disappeared under a cloud of smoke and dust. After a few more shells were fired, the roadway around the building was soon littered with broken bricks and fragments of plaster.

Six students from the Trinity OTC moved out into Great Brunswick Street (now Pearse Street) with picks and crowbars and began lifting the cobbles. With great difficulty they prised up the sets and as they lifted the last one, the side gate of

Trinity College was opened and an 18-pounder artillery piece was wheeled out from the university. The gun was anchored where the cobbled sets had been in order to prevent recoil. The weapon was zeroed in on Liberty Hall.

A squad loaded the gun and fired at the Hall, sending up a plume of smoke and dust. Peter Ennis, the caretaker of the Hall, managed to run the gauntlet of bullets and shells, escaping without injury.

The opening salvo had alerted the Volunteers to the fact that the British were launching their attack. Throughout the Volunteer posts, men grabbed their weapons and manned the barricades. At Hopkins and Hopkins (U) and Kelly's Fort (V), the Volunteers crouched behind their defences and, with a makeshift periscope, were able to witness the shelling. Soldiers rushed out from the Custom House and stormed the building, but finding the Hall empty, withdrew.

Troops from the Royal Irish Regiment moved out from Amiens Street Railway Station and fanned out into the warren of commercial and tenement buildings that stretched from Amiens Street to Sackville Street. They occupied Messrs Tuck's Engineers, Dunlop's Rubber Showrooms, the Abbey Theatre and White's Delph Store; buildings that gave them a line of fire towards the insurgent positions. They set up sniper posts and brought a number of Lewis machine guns to bear on Mansfield's Boot Shop (O) on the corner of Abbey Street and Sackville Street where Volunteers Oscar Traynor, Vincent Poole, Seán Russell and Thomas Leahy were entrenched.

The shelling was a signal for the other British positions to commence firing. The machine gunners on the roof of Trinity College opened fire on Hopkins and Hopkins (U) and Kelly's

Fort (V). The crowd of spectators on the corner of D'Olier Street and Westmorland Street scattered as they realised they were in the line of fire. Unable to return fire, the Volunteers crouched down in Hopkins and Hopkins as the walls began to disintegrate under a blizzard of bullets. The garrison in Kelly's Fort (V) opened fire with their automatic rifle towards the crew manning the gun on HMS *Helga*, forcing them to dive for cover as bullets ricocheted off the gun shield. After three bursts of automatic fire, the ammunition for the Volunteer's weapon was spent and the post ceased firing.[1]

The ANZACS on the roof of the college picked their targets and began firing, adding to the hail of bullets that were being directed towards Sackville Street. The Starry Plough flag over the Imperial Hotel was perforated as bullets tore through the standard. The Volunteers' snipers on the roof of the Dublin Bread Company (DBC) (T) could make out the zip-zip noise of incoming rounds as they sought what little cover the cupola had to offer. Bullets continued to smash into the Wireless School, sending up spurts of dust and forcing the operators to abandon their mission and take cover.

A blast of machine-gun fire cut down Volunteer Captain Thomas Weafer, who was commanding the Hibernian Bank (Q) on Lower Abbey Street. Shot through the lung, he lingered for a number of hours before succumbing to his wounds. Weafer was twenty-six years old and he left behind a widow and child.

The Volunteers on the roof of the GPO returned fire, aiming as best they could at the smoke and muzzle flashes from the attacker's rifles and machine guns. They also engaged the British troops that had taken up firing positions on the roof of the Gresham Hotel. Small squads of soldiers had infiltrated the streets north of the GPO and had taken up firing points on the roof of the Rotunda Hospital.

From his CP at the Imperial Hotel, Captain Brennan Whitmore believed that an all-out attack on the Volunteers' posts was imminent. A Vickers belt-fed machine gun was strafing the street from upper Sackville Street, its steady tock-tock-tock revealing it was firing on fixed lines.

Whitmore tried to contact the GPO by phone but found the line dead. A member of Cumann na mBán volunteered to bring a message across the bullet-swept street from the Imperial Hotel and collect vital medical supplies. She would have to cross 150 yards of exposed ground, which was being raked by enemy fire. Her hobble skirt was cut to the knee, which enabled her to run. The barricade was removed from the front door and she exited the building. Bullets kicked up vicious, vertical spurts of stone all round her, following and preceding her erratic progress. She dashed through the hail of rounds and hurled herself through the door of the GPO. Moments later, she reappeared at the door, her arms laden with supplies. With her head bowed, she ran through the gauntlet of fire once again and returned to her post. Whitmore realised that a safer method of communications would have to be established with GHQ. A ball of string was found and with one end secured at Whitmore's CP, the other end was pitched over to the GPO, secured, and then pitched back to the CP. A tin can was attached to the string and messages were placed inside the canister. However, the canister soon had a bullet hole in it, a shot that could have severed the twine. It was decided to attach just the despatch to the twine and send it across. As Whitmore was re-establishing communications with the GPO, a shell detonated at the *Freeman's Journal* building (L) in Prince's Street sent up a plume of smoke into the air. One of Whitmore's men brought the officer's attention to an enemy artillery spotter near the Parnell monument. The gun team was receiving instructions from the spotter by hand signals, which enabled the gunners to calculate the specific direction and elevation for the gun layer to point the weapon. The spotter appeared at the window and signalled. Within seconds the air was filled with the onrushing sound of an incoming round and the crunch as it impacted to the rear of GHQ. Whitmore took up a firing position and aimed his weapon at the spotter's window. As his target appeared, Whitmore fired but missed. His target, however, never reappeared.

Captain Whitmore's position was under attack from rifle fire and at least three different machine-gun positions. The Volunteers returned fire from the rooftops, but only when and where clear targets presented themselves, thus conserving their ammunition. James Connolly's forces were now fighting battles on three fronts: north, east and south of their GHQ position. Whitmore knew it would be only a matter of time before he had to extricate his force from the battlefield.

Within the GPO the members of the Provisional Government and the Republican army command sat quietly. A continuous stream of information was being exchanged between the various Volunteer posts throughout the city and GHQ. Commandant Connolly walked through the building assuring his men that the British were under pressure as they had resorted to the use of artillery and that help from the Germans was surely on the way. Despite these reassurances, the steady sound of rifle and machine-gun fire outside underlined the fact that Sackville Street had become a battleground.

Connolly left GHQ to inspect posts nearer to Abbey Street. Oscar Traynor recalled:

> We reached Eason's in Abbey Street and, although at this time heavy firing was taking place, Connolly insisted on walking out into Abbey Street and giving me instructions [as to] where I should place a barricade. While he was giving these instructions, he was standing at the edge of the path and the bullets were actually striking the pavements around us. I pointed this out to him and said I thought it was a grave risk to be taking and that these instructions could be given inside.[2]

A platoon of British soldiers crashed out through the gates of FOB Trinity and took up positions on either side of the street. They advanced cautiously towards O'Connell Bridge, scanning their arcs as they moved forward. In Kelly's Fort (V), Peader Bracken and his men brought their guns to bear and squinted down the sights. They opened fire on the advancing figures and watched as five or six men spun and collapsed on the ground. Some of the British soldiers returned fire while others in small groups were getting up, running, diving for cover and dashing forward again. Insurgent bullets were whipping past and smacking into the ground as the soldiers surged forward. Some men were shooting on the move, others halting, kneeling and taking snap shots. The artillery piece was moved into D'Olier Street and redirected to Hopkins and Hopkins (U) and Kelly's Fort (V). Volunteer Peader Bracken turned his weapon to focus on the gun crew but they took cover behind the defensive shield. A loud boom signalled the report of the gun and a sharp smack on the buildings nearby revealed the impact. The Volunteers were helpless against such adversity.

News reached Connolly by courier that the small garrison at the Mendicity Institute, which had held out for three days, had been captured. Despatches were also coming in of a major engagement at Mount Street Bridge where the British had suffered heavy casualties. While these reports boosted morale within GHQ, the Volunteer command incorrectly believed that the artillery strikes were being used to soften up the Volunteer positions before an infantry assault was launched from the south of the river, a move that Connolly would make very costly for the British.

Later that evening, the garrison in Hopkins and Hopkins received an order to pull out. The men evacuated the building and pulled back to reinforce the Volunteers within Clery's/Imperial Hotel (J). The DBC (T) was also vacated at this time, leaving all the posts from Abbey Street to the quays empty. Kelly's Fort (V) had also been vacated on orders from James Connolly. Both units pulled out through the maze of mouse-holes that had been bored from building to building. Two Volunteer outer-defensive posts had been vacated, leaving the bridgehead undefended.

As the rifle fire subsided for the night, the Volunteers dossed down and tried to get some rest. The first day of fighting had been nerve-wracking for the Volunteers who had never been under artillery fire before. Lit cigarettes were passed from hand to shaded hand. Many tried to catch some sleep while others snatched some food. The noose was slowly beginning to tighten.

Chapter 9

Thursday, 27 April 1916: Morning

THE DARK OF THE DAWN

At 00.30 hours, an improvised armoured personnel carrier (APC) trundled onto Sackville Street and drove towards the Gresham Hotel. The driver was squeezed into the truck behind the steering wheel, a position that was equivalent to being in an armoured kiln. The soldiers of the Royal Irish Regiment (RIR) in the rear of the vehicle could hardly communicate over the din of the shooting outside. The rattle of bullets and the dissonant irregular ping when they made contact with the metal deafened those inside. Pulling up outside the hotel, the back doors were thrown open and twenty soldiers sprang from back of the APC and ran into the building. In order to operate in areas dominated by rebel fire, a retired colonel, Henry T. W. Allatt of the Royal Irish Rifles, had devised the idea of fitting a number of flat-bed Daimler Lorries with large boilers that had been supplied by the Guinness Brewery. In order to protect the driver, the cab of the lorry had been armoured with heavy steel plating. He was able to drive the vehicle by looking through a small slit in the plating. Loop holes were drilled in the sides of the boiler on the lorry-bed, providing firing slits for the troops in the back. Initially used for reconnaissance in the city, the APCs were now being used to manoeuvre troops into position.

As the APC began to move off, Volunteer Joe Sweeny took aim at the driver's slit in the armoured car and opened fire. The APC slewed across the road and shuddered to a halt. The vehicle remained there for a number of hours under continuous fire from the Volunteers on the GPO roof until another APC arrived and towed the stricken vehicle out of the kill zone.

The British troops that had entered the Gresham Hotel took up firing positions on the upper floors. Targeting the GPO, the soldiers worked the bolts of their weapons furiously as streams of cartridge cases poured from their rifles onto the floor. Belts of cartridge cases tore through the hands of the machine gunners. Ejected cases spun from the smoking breeches and orange flames spat from their muzzles as the gunners traversed their weapons. The Volunteers within the GPO took cover as the frontage of the building disintegrated under a cloud of dust as bullets tore its edifice:

> Every machine gun within range began to pour in a fierce fire upon the area and every soldier, including the British snipers, joined in with rapid rifle fire. The torrent of bullets on and around our field headquarters could only be compared to a violent hailstorm.[1]

General Lowe needed to prepare his proposed battleground carefully, for he knew that if he went straight into the first major phase of the operation without conducting some type of clearance or shaping the area first, he would take a serious number of casualties. He deployed his reinforcements which had arrived as part of the 59th Division as follows: the 2/4 Lincolns were ordered to establish an outer cordon around the southern suburbs of the city. The 2/5th and 2/6th South Staffordshire Regiments were ordered to attack the Four Courts area while the Nottingham and Derbyshire Regiments (Sherwood Foresters) and the Irish Regiments were to take care of the rebel headquarters on Sackville Street. Thousands of soldiers of the South and North Staffordshire Regiments and the Sherwood Foresters had moved through Trinity College on their way to Dublin Castle, where they prepared to launch an assault on the city.

The shelling recommenced south of the river with the gunners zeroing in on rebel positions near the GPO. The first shell crashed into the *Irish Times* printing office on Lower Abbey Street, igniting the newspaper rolls. Huge flames leaped from the building and the fire spread rapidly through the street. The barricade of newsprint rolls and furniture erected by Thomas Weafer's section caught fire, allowing the conflagration to spread. Fires were now blazing in Sackville Place and Lower Abbey Street, including at Wynn's Hotel. Incendiary, shrapnel and high-explosive shells rained in on the Volunteer positions.

> There were shrapnel shells, and the amazing thing was that instead of bullets coming in it was molten lead, actually molten, which streamed about on the ground when it fell. I was told that the shrapnel was filled with molten wax, the bullets were embedded in wax, and the

velocity of the shell through the barrel and through the air caused the mould to melt. As the first of these shells hit the house, the Volunteers rushed and told me about them. I rushed up and found an old fellow crawling about on his hands and knees gathering the stuff up as it hardened. I asked him what he was doing and what he intended to do with the stuff. He said, 'Souvenirs'.[2]

From his position in Mansfield Boot Makers (O), Oscar Traynor and his men were heavily engaged with British forces.

So continuous was their rate of fire at this time that the barrels of the rifles became overheated. It was then that Captain Poole, who had served in the British Army and in the South African campaign, proposed that, in the absence of any suitable oil for cooling the rifles, we should open some sardine tins and use this oil. This was done, with the result that the men were able to continue in action.[3]

Machine-gun fire splintered the wooden window frames and sent clouds of brick and plaster dust into the air. The Volunteers crawled along the floors avoiding the gunfire, only raising themselves to return fire when the machine gunner paused to change belts.

British soldiers moved cautiously up Westmorland Street and D'Olier Street, taking up firing positions in the buildings overlooking O'Connell Bridge.

North of the battleground, the 3rd Battalion of the Royal Irish Regiment set up Battalion Headquarters in the National

Bank on the corner of Great Brunswick Street and Sackville Street. From here, the officer commanding directed his men to secure the area. A platoon of picked shots under Major J. D. Morrough (RIR) succeeded in obtaining advantageous sniping positions on the roofs and opened fire on the post office. An APC was used to tow a field gun into position at the top of Sackville Street, which opened fire on the GPO and the surrounding buildings.

Mick Boland and Liam Tannam were on the roof of the GPO when the first shell impacted. There was a silence, as if the crack of the explosives had sucked all the sound out of the air. Boland's face was covered in blood from where he had been hit by shrapnel. Machine-gun rounds kicked up dust from the building's ornate parapet, sending shards of stone into the air and British troops began pouring fire into the GPO – it was the beginning of the end.

Chapter 10

Thursday, 27 April 1916: Afternoon

BLOOD AND EMBERS

Commandant James Connolly, weary from hours of inspecting his posts, moved from room to room within the General Post Office, ordering his men to reinforce the defences as he believed that a British infantry attack was imminent. He ordered a redoubt to be built within the main hall: mail sacks were filled with coal from the cellars and the makeshift defences were piled high. A platoon of Volunteers took up position behind the sacks in readiness for an assault.

Volunteer Eamon Dore managed to break through the British lines on Great Britain Street and report to the GPO. Meeting Tom Clarke, he suggested that it would be possible to take a section of men and work around behind the military line at the top of Sackville Street and launch an attack from behind the British lines. Tom Clarke replied: 'We have no authority. Connolly is in charge here and we will report what you have said.' However, this plan was never executed.[1]

Commandant Connolly was busy reinforcing his defences, having realised that an enemy attack launched from Capel Street would wreak havoc on the rear of his position. Assembling a section of Volunteers, Connolly moved out of the GPO and headed down Henry Street towards the junction with Liffey Street. The air crackled with bullets as they edged their way along the street. Connolly divided the group into two: the first squad occupying a warehouse, the second group occupying O'Neill's public house in Liffey Street. These posts covered the approaches to Mary Street and Denmark Street. As Connolly was examining the positions, he was shot and wounded, the bullet piercing his upper right arm. Without allowing his command to know that he had been wounded, Connolly made his way back to the GPO where James Ryan dressed the wound. The medic was ordered not to mention the incident to anyone and the officer continued with his rounds.

A shout of 'stand to' echoed through the GPO as one of the APCs attempted to drive up Henry Street, probing the Volunteer defences. From the roof of the warehouse, Volunteer John Reid got comfortable in the prone position next to his colleagues and calmly started to lay down a number of rounds against the APC. Bullets were making a ping and tink sound as they bounced off the plating on the vehicle. A bomb was thrown from a rooftop, and the explosion forced the vehicle to withdraw.

Commandant Connolly realised that British forces would launch an assault from both ends of Abbey Street: from Lower Abbey Street at one end and from one of the many bridges over the River Liffey at the other. A platoon was assembled in the main hall of the GPO and Connolly ordered John

Macloughlin to take charge and cover the small units in Liffey Street and Henry Street by occupying the *Irish Independent* offices on Abbey Street.

The platoon moved off with Connolly following them out of the GPO into Prince's Street and then on to Abbey Street. Rifle and machine-gun bullets cut through the air as the group advanced. Ten men occupied Lucas's Lamp Shop while the remainder dashed out from cover and ran towards the *Independent* offices. As Connolly prepared to retrace his steps back to headquarters, a shot ricocheted off the pavement, hitting him in the ankle. Collapsing to the ground and writhing in agony, the wounded officer dragged himself to cover, leaving a thick trail of blood in his wake. Connolly began crawling back to Prince's Street, a painstakingly slow and agonising process. When he finally reached the street, his men picked him up and carried him into the building where his wound was dressed. In agony, the officer was given frequent injections of morphine to stem the pain. The O'Rahilly assumed command of the Republican Army with the support of Clarke and MacDermott, who became more assertive. Pearse continued to encourage the men but the effects of sleep deprivation were beginning to show, not only on the leaders, but on all the Volunteers within GHQ.

From the Metropole Hotel (M), Volunteer Oscar Traynor witnessed the devastation caused by the shelling:

Some time on Thursday a barricade, which stretched from the Royal Hibernian Academy to a cycle shop [J. J. Keating's] ... on the opposite side of the street, took fire as a result of a direct shell hit. It was the firing of this barricade that caused the fire, which wiped out the east side of O'Connell Street. I saw that happen myself. I saw the barricade being hit; I saw the fire consuming it and I saw Keating's going up. Then Hoyte's caught fire, and when Hoyte's caught fire the whole block up to Earl Street became involved. Hoyte's had a lot of turpentine and other inflammable stuff, and I saw the fire spread from there to Clery's. Clery's and the Imperial Hotel were one and the same building, and this building was ignited from the fire which consumed Hoyte's ... I had the extraordinary experience of seeing the huge plate-glass windows of Clery's stores run molten into the channel from the terrific heat.[2]

The fires extended from Clery's/Imperial Hotel (J) down to Hopkin's corner on the quays. Across the street, the fires had engulfed the buildings from the Metropole Hotel (M) down to Carlisle Bridge. The beleaguered garrison within Clery's/Imperial Hotel (J) continued to hold out.

Volunteer Kevin McCabe attempted to contact the fire brigade:

In my simplicity I took up the phone to speak to the Fire Brigade. I was answered, rather to my surprise and was asked where I was speaking from. I said, 'You must not ask too many questions' and was then told that they intended to let us burn out.[3]

Each exploding artillery shell rearranged the rubble, blasting pieces into the air and creating clouds of pulverized brick dust. The Volunteers were powerless and could do nothing but shelter, crouching as low as they could behind their make-shift barricades. They waited with bated breath, anticipating the next explosion. Having been ordered to hold the building until it was impossible for the enemy to occupy it, Volunteer Frank Henderson ordered his men to move before they were all killed. The Volunteers passed the word 'we're pulling out' down the line. The men crawled to the exit and prepared to leave the burning building:

> ...we remained until the ceiling of the first floor was falling all around us in flames and then retreated through Allen's, which was now one huge wall of flames. We had to come down a ladder about fifteen feet which was on fire, and gradually worked our way out, having received severe burns ...[4]

Though the Volunteers were outside, they were on the opposite side of the street to where GHQ was located. Artillery and small-arms fire began falling around the buildings, the noise amplified by the narrow streets. Scouring their flanks and breathing in short shallow gasps, the group made their way to Gloucester Street where they found refuge in an abandoned house. In an attempt to reconnoitre the area, Volunteer Patrick O'Connor was shot and killed. He was a native of Rathmore in County Kerry.

As the flames engulfed the hotel, four men stumbled out through the main door. A small rearguard, having denied the building to the enemy, was now withdrawing from their post. Long bursts of machine-gun fire cut through the air as shells screamed overhead, all adding to the cacophony. Signalling to the Volunteers in GHQ that they intended to cross the bullet-swept street, the squad made ready. The main doors of the post office were thrown open to receive them and amid the din and smoke of battle, they raced across the road one by one. Machine-gunners traversed their weapons in an attempt to pick them off but to no avail. The smoke screen shielded them from view, all but the last man who had wrapped himself in a mattress to run the gauntlet of fire. As he ran, rounds struck the ground by his feet. He slipped and fell, feigning death, as the gunner traversed his weapon. Jumping up to cheers from the GPO garrison, he continued his dash and reached the safety of the post office. Ten minutes later, the windows of the hotel were blown out.

With the fires spreading and the buildings under constant rifle, artillery and machine-gun fire, Captain Brennan Whitmore had no option but to pull out of his position on North Earl Street and attempt to get to Fairview on the north side of the city. He relayed some quick battle orders to the assembled group before they made ready to evacuate their posts. As they were unable to traverse Sackville Street, Whitmore decided to extricate his force across North Earl Street and by using a series of back lanes, old mews and alleyways, they would come out onto Cathedral Street and then onto Marlborough Street. As they opened the doors, the air outside was thick with smoke from the burning buildings and the smell of cordite from the British guns. The group zig-zagged across the road and ran a few hundred metres, stopping every fifty metres or so to catch their breath and scan their arcs across the deserted streets. They could hear the sound of battle all around them as the thumping of the British guns and the crashing crack of shell impacts resounded throughout the city. As they made their way through the smoke and carnage, Whitmore decided to leave the female members of his group at a Presbytery near Marlborough Street. They objected strongly to being left behind and remonstrated with Whitmore, but to no avail. The group continued on until challenged by British troops. A number of shots were fired and Whitmore and another man were both wounded. The Volunteers took refuge in the basement of one of the many tenement buildings in the area and made ready for a British attack. Though an attack did not materialise, Whitmore posted sentries on the building and settled down to try and figure out a way to break through the British cordon.

The fear of every Volunteer was that if they were captured they would be summarily executed. The small groups of Volunteers that had managed to evade capture were adamant that they would break out and regroup in the north of the city.

Officers of the Sherwood Foresters assembled in the operations room of Dublin Castle and were briefed on General Lowe's plan to retake the city. As the briefing closed, all officers knew their routes towards the areas of operation. Outside, hundreds of heavily laden soldiers waited tensely for the order to move. Having been held in reserve for most of the day, the Sherwood Foresters were at last cleared to launch their attack. Zero hour was 17.00 hours.

Chapter 11

Thursday, 27 April 1916: Evening

ARC OF FIRE

At 17.00 hours, the first units of the 2/6th Sherwood Foresters moved out from Dublin Castle. Their objective was to secure and occupy Capel Street. Under fire from the Four Courts, an armoured personnel carrier (APC) drove at high speed across Grattan Bridge and into Capel Street. A section debussed from the vehicle and took up firing positions in a corner building, giving the Sherwood Foresters a good field of fire which could be brought to bear in either direction. The APC accelerated up the street and deposited the remainder of the soldiers. Under fire from insurgent snipers, the military began clearing the many tenement houses on the street.

A signal was relayed back to the Castle that the street had been taken and secured. A platoon of Sherwood Foresters, lying in the prone position in Parliament Street, waited patiently on the order to move. On the shrill blast of a whistle, they proceeded to move at the double across Grattan Bridge, which was under heavy fire from the Four Courts. As they set off on a crouching run, bullets struck the parapet and tram lines and ricocheted, throwing sparks in all directions. On arriving in Capel Street, the platoon was ordered into a defensive circle. A corner house was designated as a Command Post (CP) where the officers congregated for a briefing. Impeded by their lack of knowledge of the area, a sergeant was detailed to find a map. He located one in an abandoned newspaper office.

The officers immediately set about deploying their forces in the area. Each company of the Sherwood Foresters was allocated a fixed area to clear, and each platoon or section was then assigned a building or street to secure in that area. Captain Edmunds with 'A' Company secured a sector from Capel Street to Coles Lane, while 'C' Company, under Captain Jackson, was made responsible for securing Upper Abbey and Liffey Streets. 'D' Company, under the command of Captain Tomkins, was ordered to secure the area from Coles Lane to Sackville Street and Captain Orr, commanding 'B' Company, was ordered to contain the Four Courts. The map also revealed a soap factory where the military commandeered a number of empty sacks, which were then filled with earth from the floors of the tenement houses. The sandbags were used to reinforce their posts, making the street a secure highway for the Staffordshire Regiment who were to begin operations later that night on North King Street. A second platoon of Sherwood Foresters pushed through Capel Street and into Great Britain Street (Parnell Street) linking up with the Royal Irish Regiment who were holding the area.

A British reconnaissance patrol fanned out into their assault posture and advanced steadily towards their objective. They manoeuvred carefully out of Great Britain Street and advanced into Moore Street in an attempt to probe the Volunteer defences. Within minutes, a bitter street fight had erupted among the debris-strewn streets. Gunfire erupted from a number of posts causing the patrol to fall back. Volunteer Seán Nunan recalled:

> On the far side of Moore Street, a British soldier was lying, badly wounded in the stomach and calling for help. Despite the fact that the street was swept by machine-gun fire from the Parnell Street [Great Britain Street] end, George Plunkett took a water bottle from a man alongside me, crossed Moore Street, gave the soldier a drink and then carried him back to our head-quarters.[1]

Nancy Wyse Power noted that:

> From the high ground at the top of Parnell Square I saw a procession of women bearing a white flag crossing O'Connell Street at the Parnell monument. These were inhabitants of the Moore Street Parnell Street area leaving their homes for safety.[2]

While many residents evacuated the area, others decided to remain.

British snipers on the roof of the Gresham Hotel continued to fire into the GPO; men and women crouched behind the makeshift defences avoiding the hail of bullets. On the roof of the GPO, Volunteer Dick Humphries devised a plan to eliminate the threat:

> We allow them to continue firing until, mystified at our silence, they grow bolder, and incautiously show themselves over the top of the parapet. Immediately a single volley rings out. There was no more sniping that evening from the Gresham.[3]

Gun battles continued in the surrounding streets as the high-pitched clatter of rifles, the boom of the artillery and the relentless machine-gun fire continued into the night. On the roof of Trinity College, machine-gunners continually identified and engaged targets.

Volunteer Thomas O'Reilly was shot dead in the vicinity of the GPO. He was taken to Jervis Street Hospital where he was pronounced dead. Thomas O'Reilly was twenty-two years old and a member of the Irish Citizen Army.

The east side of Sackville Street was a mass of flame and smoke. The heat from the fires spread across to the GPO and the garrison had to break out fire hoses and spray their barricades in order to stop them from igniting. The Volunteers could only shoot at the shadows which darted in and out of the side streets. British troops continued to fire on the building, which was now illuminated by the fires which surrounded it. Within the GPO, Pearse walked through the building encouraging his men. Despite the loss of communications with the other posts in Dublin, despite the fires and despite knowing that no relief was forthcoming, he knew that the Irish Republican Army still held GHQ on the main street of Dublin city and had done so for four days.

Sackville Street burned throughout the evening. At 19.30 hours, the façade of the Waverly Hotel collapsed into the street, followed soon after by Hopkins and Hopkins (U). The DBC (T) and Reis's (R) followed suit; the walls of flames, the acrid smoke and the noise of the crumbling buildings being ripped from the city's skyline.

The machine-gun fire and the shelling subsided and only the sound of desultory rifle fire could be heard throughout the city. At 22.00 hours, Hoyte's (P) exploded in a ball of flames. From his vantage point in the GPO, Volunteer Patrick Colgan later wrote:

> Hoyte's chemist shop was a most attractive sight with globular fire balls rising into the skies and dying out. The glass tower of the D.B.C. restaurant was also an attractive fire. The flames licking up the glass tower, dying out, the tower twisting and bending and finally collapsing.[4]

The ground shuddered as hundreds of oil drums stored behind Hoyte's (P) exploded in a massive fireball, which lit up the night sky. The heat from the explosion struck the Volunteers in the GPO, who worked their fire hoses furiously to keep their defences from catching fire. Charles Saurin wrote:

> The heat from the burning block opposite the G.P.O. was beyond belief. Despite the great width of O'Connell Street the sacks, etc. in the windows began to scorch and show signs of smouldering. Batches of men had to be

Sackville Street with Nelson's Pillar (Kieran Delany)

The General Post Office, Sackville Street, circa 1916
(Kieran Delany)

The corner of Sackville Street and Abbey Street after
the Rising (Author's Collection)

The newly refurbished GPO, weeks before the Rising erupted
(James Langton)

The interior of the GPO after the insurrection (Kilmainham Gaol)

The O'Rahilly
(James Langton)

Volunteers inside the GPO during Easter week, 1916 (Kilmainham Gaol)

A British field kitchen in the grounds of Trinity College (Irish Regiments)

A British machine gun unit (Author's collection)

A British .303 Vickers machine gun and crew (Author's collection)

The devastation caused by artillery on Sackville Street (Kilmainham Gaol)

Ruins of the GPO from the top of Nelson's Pillar (Kilmainham Gaol)

The ruins of the Metropole Hotel (Kilmainham Gaol)

Henry Street (David Smith)

Kelly's Fort (Kilmainham Gaol)

British soldiers display the captured republican flag (Irish Regiments)

Sackville Street in flames (Daily Sketch)

Stonebreakers yard, Kilmainham
Gaol (Author's Collection)

hastily formed to continually drench the window fortifications with water. Dense volumes of acrid smoke,
myriads of sparks and splinters of falling debris were
being blown to the G.P.O. by a strong north-east wind.
Lurid flames leapt skywards and the spectacle in the
gathering darkness could only be likened to Dante's
Inferno. The intensity of the heat grew steadily worse and
the water being poured from buckets and hoses was con-
verted into steam as it touched the fortifications. There
had to be a withdrawal from the front of the building of
all save those who were combating the risk of conflagration in the Post Office itself. Our struggle with this new
danger seemed to go on for interminable hours. The
men were soot-stained, steam-scalded and fire-scorched,
sweating, weary and parched.[5]

From their many vantage points throughout the city, soldiers
from both sides watched as a million sparks illuminated the
night sky. Dublin city was burning.

Chapter 12

Friday, 28 April 1916: Morning

THE CRUCIBLE

At 02.00 hours, General Sir John Grenfell Maxwell, KCB, KCMG, and his staff arrived in Dublin Port. As they stepped from the gangplank onto Irish soil, the city of Dublin was in flames. Machine-gun and small-arms fire cracked throughout the city and clouds of cordite drifted across the River Liffey as Maxwell travelled by motor car to the Royal Hospital in Kilmainham. On arrival, the officers were given a situation report by General Lowe. As the officers' briefing was taking place, British troops were tightening the cordon around the Volunteers' positions. Maxwell confirmed Lowe's plan to retake the city and deployed the 2/4th Lincolns (part of the 176th Brigade, which had just arrived in Dublin, bringing the 59th Division to its full complement) to set up an outer cordon around the city.[1]

The 5th Leinsters, the Dublin Fusiliers, the Ulster Composite Battalion along with the troops of the mobile column held a line that stretched from Dublin Castle through Dame Street to Trinity College and on to the Custom House, into Amiens Street Station and up Gardiner Street. On Great Britain Street, the Royal Irish Regiment had secured the immediate area.

Speed was of the essence as the Sherwood Foresters surged forward into the labyrinth of streets to the rear of the GPO. Captain Jackson's 'C' Company pushed in from Capel Street towards Abbey Street while 'A' Company cleared Jervis Street and Denmark Street. 'B' Company moved a field gun into position on Great Britain Street at the junction with Cole's Lane, cutting off any possible escape routes for the insurgents. British forces also brought a number of light trench-mortars into position around the post office.[2] This new and surprisingly simple weapon comprised a smooth bore tube fixed to a base plate and a lightweight bipod. The weapon was fired by dropping a ten-pound mortar round down the barrel, which caused a striking pin at the bottom of the tube to ignite a 12-bore cartridge at the base of the mortar round. The cartridge ignited a propellant charge, which then sent the mortar along a predetermined trajectory towards the Irish positions. The weapon had a high rate of fire and had an effective range of 750 yards.[3] Machine-gun teams were deployed to the area, taking up position on rooftops dominating the battleground.

At 06.00 hours the attack went in. A barrage of artillery and mortar fire burst with drumfire crumps and an irregular series of white flashes, like sheet lightening. Machine-gun and rifle fire added to the noise of battle. Explosions illuminated the ground through dense clouds of reeking cordite and dust that billowed up into the black sky.

In the streets at the back of the GPO, the Sherwood Foresters made ready to assault the defensive perimeter to the rear of the Volunteer lines. A mortar team dropped a high-explosive round down the muzzle of their weapon. The men ducked away, covering their ears. There was a split second of metal scraping against metal as the bomb slid down onto the firing pin. The morning sky exploded as a sudden series of crumps and flashes heralded the beginning of a mortar barrage. The sound echoed off the walls of the narrow streets as the Volunteers manned their posts. Within seconds the Sherwood Foresters surged forwards. Automatic fire zipped above and around the republican positions. The Volunteers returned fire and soon there were innumerable spent brass cartridge cases littering the floors of the strong points. The Volunteers coughed and tried to cover their faces to stop the acrid smell of cordite that drifted back into the room. The Sherwood Foresters continued their advance:

'A' Company was ordered to clear Denmark Street. At the bottom of this street was O'Neill's public house. From this house we had sustained considerable sniping. A section was told to keep down the fire from this public house. Then the house was rushed, but the enemy had fled, leaving pools of blood and traces of the damage we had done to some of their snipers. Carefully searching all the houses as we pushed on, we found a rabbit warren of alleys on the east side. The women were incoherent with fear and what with hysterical women, screeching children and the unpleasant task of searching the filthiest houses one had ever seen, the task was anything but pleasant. No arms were found and few men. The reason was clear. All the rows of houses in this area had been connected by holes knocked into the dividing walls, so the rebels could get from one end to the other without being observed. The public house was provisioned for a siege and the numerous empty shells testified to the amount of sniping that had gone on.[4]

Houses continued to be cleared amid the gunfire as British forces consolidated and gradually contracted the cordon round the GPO.

A civilian, G. F. H. Heenan, entered in his diary:

There was very severe fighting throughout the streets of Dublin last night and we could see the different fires in different parts of the city and hear the boom of the guns and the rattle of machine-gun fire. It is stated that the losses on both sides yesterday were very heavy and that the government troops were driving the rebels back steadily from many of the streets, but that they still hold most of the large buildings that they occupied on Monday last. This house-to-house fighting is dreadful, and hundreds of innocent men, women and children are being sacrificed, all for national or party madness.[5]

The inexperienced British soldiers found themselves fighting for their lives in the streets of the city. Private James W. Woods of the 2/7th Sherwood Foresters later wrote:

Really, we are lucky to be able to tell the tale, as no sooner had we halted and got down ready when we were fired on from all quarters. We retired for a few yards amidst a veritable hail of bullets. The worst part of the job was [that] we did not know who our enemy were, with the result that we had to be careful when we fired. Shots were coming from out of the windows, off roofs and behind chimneys. The enemy were very artful, as, when they had fired a shot from a window they would put a little child in the position they had occupied. Rifle fire was not much use, so our officer took parties and rushed the suspected house with fixed bayonets. This was very successful. One of our corporals saw some men on a roof, and went up single handed and fetched them down. They numbered seven. He also conducted bombing parties, and did very good work. If it had not been for bombs we should not have done so well.[6]

In Henry Street, civilians – some intent on looting, others trying to escape the carnage – ran into the conflagrations. Many were caught in the crossfire and shot down in the street. Sackville Street was an inferno, with buildings burning and collapsing into the street. The Volunteers could hear the fall of masonry as shells impacted on their targets. A mix of grey and black smoke hung over the city like a shroud.

Troops in Westmorland Street pushed forward under the cover of artillery fire. The Volunteers in the Metropole Hotel (M) and the block of buildings adjacent fired at the advancing soldiers, forcing them to halt their attack and take up position at the bridge head. In trying to gauge the distance to the GPO, the gun crew fired over open sights and hit the Metropole Hotel (M). The shrapnel shells exploded harmlessly, scattering their payload over the roof and little showers of plaster dust descended from the ceiling. Inside the hotel, the Volunteers knelt by the windows, a position that gave them a perfect spot to fire from, with good cover from the blizzard of bullets. Oscar Traynor and his men held the corner building, preventing the British from advancing up Lower Abbey Street and also preventing an attack from across Carlisle Bridge. British machine guns opened fire from the building at the division of Westmorland and D'Olier Streets. Word reached the group that they were to evacuate and return to GHQ. On returning, however, Pearse stated that no order had been issued to pull out and that it was imperative that the block of buildings be held in order to give protection to the post office. Oscar Traynor and his men returned to their position and once again manned their posts.

As the barrage of shells rained down and moved nearer the Volunteer positions, Pearse, Connolly, Clarke, Plunkett and MacDermott held an officers' briefing. The situation had deteriorated rapidly within the last twenty-four hours. The British were not prepared to launch a frontal assault on the GPO and were not conducting operations as the Volunteers had anticipated. It was now apparent that they intended to devastate Volunteer posts and Sackville Street with artillery fire. Communications had been severed with all of the outlying republican positions. British forces had also driven a wedge between the Four Courts and GHQ, cutting off any possible escape route to north county Dublin. Headquarters were effectively surrounded and with the continuous shelling, the garrison would have to break out, regroup and strategize. If they could hold out until nightfall they could use the cover of darkness to extricate their forces from the building and move them to a new position. The route to the target building would have to be secured before the main force could pull out. The sewers were considered as an escape route but were found to be impassable on inspection. The alternative was to move out into the streets – under fire. Identifying a suitable post within the vicinity to be secured and held was the next dilemma facing the Volunteer command.

Captain Brennan Whitmore, who had managed to extricate his force from North Earl Street and had taken refuge in a tenement building, awoke to the shouts of 'Hands up!' by British soldiers standing in the doorway, their rifles levelled at the Volunteers. The room was dark and amid the noise and confusion Whitmore fired his weapon, the bullet passing through the sleeve of a young British Lieutenant. He was incensed and an argument ensued between the officer and the Volunteer who had fired the shot. A sergeant pushed his way into the room and momentarily defused the tense situation.

The Volunteers were ushered outside at the point of a bayonet, lined up and threatened to be shot by the angry officer. A loud cheer went up from the onlookers who bayed for blood. As the scene was unfolding, a captain arrived, and having listened to the lieutenant's version of events, ordered the sergeant to escort the prisoners to the Custom House. Outnumbered and outgunned, Whitmore and his men were marched into captivity. Held under guard, the Volunteers watched as other small batches of prisoners arrived at the Custom House. With the intensity of the fighting, the smoke and the confusion, many of the units had managed to withdraw from the battle. They had hoped to establish contact when the day dawned but had found themselves hopelessly cut off and surrounded by superior forces. Every republican post was now surrounded, cut off and fighting for survival.

Chapter 13

Friday, 28 April 1916: Afternoon

A RING OF FIRE AND STEEL

At 13.00 hours, the snipers on the roof of the General Post Office were ordered to relinquish their position and return to the main hall. As they crawled along on their hands and knees, the air fizzed and crackled with bullets. There seemed to be no space between them as they passed overhead. Rounds were smacking into the building, showering the defenders in dust as they climbed down the ropes into the GPO.

British artillery observers were attempting to zero in on the post office. Through their binoculars they observed the number of hits on and around their target. Plumes of smoke rose into the sky as the mighty concussion of the guns reverberated through the city. Prisoners within the GPO were removed from the main area and placed under guard in the basement, as were the remainder of the ammunition supplies and explosive devices. An interior breastwork of mail bags filled with coal was constructed to the right of the main entrance in the event of the building being rushed and a section was withdrawn from the Coliseum (G) to reinforce this interior position.

At 16.00 hours an artillery officer shouted, 'Direct fire, open sights, range 350 yards, fire.' Shells shrieked overhead, hitting the GPO and sending up plumes of smoke and debris. Having determined the range and cleared all obstacles, artillery observers were now concentrating on the rebel headquarters. High-explosive, shrapnel and incendiary shells crashed onto the roof of the GPO. Splashes of dust and shards of hot metal cut through the air. Rills of smoke rose from the tiny holes where the razor-sharp shrapnel had cut into the stonework. The roof parapet was raked with machine-gun fire.

Eamon Bulfin recalled:

I remember distinctly the Post Office being hit by shells. We were informed that the floor above us was made of ferro concrete and that there was absolutely no danger of the floor coming down.[1]

Fire hoses were reeled out and jets of water were directed onto the fires that seemed to spring up throughout the building. Water gushed onto the flames but was ultimately futile, for as soon as one fire was extinguished another one appeared. The heat was intense as the Volunteers dropped their weapons to man the hoses and men formed several bucket lines to pass the water along with great urgency. As each shell impacted, the building shook and another fire appeared. The death knell struck when an incendiary shell struck the portico. The flame spread from above and gradually moved down the lift shafts to the cellars. Volunteer Tom Harris, who was on duty in the Instrument Room, later wrote:

I remember being in the Instrument Room where it was first noticed that the Post Office was on fire. The ceilings were arched. You could hear the guns going and I saw a little hole, just a circle, which came in the plaster, about the circumference of a teacup, and I could see this growing larger. It was evidently caused by an incendiary bomb.[2]

Pearse, with the assistance of the O'Rahilly, split the garrison in two, with one half dealing with the fires while the other was ordered to remain at their posts and defend against an enemy attack. Working parties immediately began hauling ladders into position and began breaking through the ceiling with pickaxes and hammers. Hoses were aimed through the apertures and directed onto the flames. Working amidst the horrific conditions, the men toiled heroically to douse the flames and save their position. Bullets came through the windows and sliced through the air as the men worked frantically to bring the fires under control. Bullets smacked into the sandbags stacked up around the windows.

The place was now an inferno. Some of our men were hosing the flames that had spread along the roof, and between the flames, the smoke and the water dripping down on us, we didn't feel very comfortable. Still, we made the welkin ring with rousing song and chorus, just to keep our spirits up.[3]

At the loop-holed positions, Volunteers scoured the streetscape looking for targets. On locating an enemy post, they took careful aim and returned fire. Boxes of ammunition were dragged along the floor to the various firing points, their contents distributed to the men. Bullets continued to crackle from the British posts across the street.

At 18.00 hours it was decided to evacuate the wounded from GHQ to Jervis Street Hospital along with a number of the Cumann na mBán. On being told that they were being ordered to evacuate, the women remonstrated with the officers. Connolly's secretary, Winifred Carney, refused to leave and insisted on remaining with him. Two others, Julia Grennan and Elizabeth O'Farrell, also remained with the GPO garrison.

The group consisting of Fr John Flanagan, Captain Mahony, sixteen wounded Volunteers, twelve women and a number of stretcher-bearers hastily assembled in the hall where Pearse addressed the contingent. He assured them that they deserved a foremost place in the nation's history and that their devotion and bravery would be remembered. He shook each of them by hand and bid them farewell. The group, led by Fr Flanagan, crawled through the tunnelled walls of the intervening houses, across a roof, up a ladder and into the Coliseum Theatre (G) where the group took cover and had a brief respite before determining the remainder of their route.

British tactical assault teams pushed forward into Abbey Street and advanced cautiously into Sackville Street. Sustained rifle and machine-gun fire was directed onto the Metropole-Mansfield posts, which, which caught fire after being hit by a number of shells. Within a short while the buildings were an inferno. Having escaped from burning stables, maddened horses rushed through Abbey Street. The shops and hotel had become untenable and the small garrison was ordered to fall back to the GPO. Moving through the labyrinth of tunnels that linked the positions, the group withdrew and crossed Prince's Street and into the GPO without any casualties.

Outside, the Sherwood Foresters' advance to the rear of the GPO was stalled as they met withering fire from republican posts. As the Volunteers' defensive perimeter slowly contracted, the boom of explosions and the crackle of small arms fire filled the air:

> The rebels used dum-dum bullets and they had a few bombs. Our bombers were sent to work and house after house was blown up. Pianos etc flew up like rockets. Sackville Street, one of the finest streets in the world, was ruined. Two officers who had been to the front said that France was heaven compared with this. One of my pals was wounded, and has since died.[4]

The Foresters and the Royal Irish Regiment reinforced their posts in the area and constructed a number of barricades which blocked the roads. A Rolls-Royce armoured car came to a sudden halt near Moore Street and traversed its turret and opened fire with its water-cooled Vickers .303 machine gun. Bullets ricocheted off the walls, crashing through the windows of the houses on the street. The terrified residents, having endured days of shelling and rifle fire, crouched down on the floor as their homes were shot to pieces.

The British prisoners, who had been held captive since Monday, were ushered at gunpoint from the fiery basement to an upper yard where they were told to make a run for it.

As the door of the GPO onto Henry Street was thrown open, the prisoners scrambled to get clear of the inferno and ran for their lives into the bullet-swept streets. Running the gauntlet of machine-gun and rifle fire, a number of the fleeing men were gunned down. Though badly wounded, some managed to find cover amongst the ruins of Dublin city.

Within the GPO, Pearse and Connolly convened with Clarke, Plunkett and MacDermott and decided to extract themselves from their position. The Irish pocket had gradually retracted and with many outposts being evacuated, the GPO was under constant artillery fire. Messrs. William's and Wood's, Soap and Sweet Manufacturers, located in Great Britain Street, was identified as a suitable fall-back position. If they were able to break through the British lines, occupy the building and hold out, the British would be forced to cease fire as they risked shelling their own men. By holding onto the enemy's belt buckle, the Volunteers could establish a new defensive perimeter, which would give them some respite from the devastating artillery fire. In order to provide a safe passage from Henry Street and up Moore Street to the target building, the route would have to be secured. The O'Rahilly volunteered to lead the mission.

> I heard the O'Rahilly calling for twenty men with bayonets to make a charge. There was not a very prompt response to his call, which seemed reasonable to me, because what or whom he was going to charge was not clear…O'Rahilly shouted, 'Are you Irishmen that you won't charge?' and the men stepped forward more promptly.[5]

A platoon was hastily assembled and the men locked and loaded their weapons and fixed bayonets. Unholstering his automatic pistol, the O'Rahilly and his group filtered out into the fire and smoke of Henry Street and disappeared into the maelstrom.

Chapter 14

Friday, 28 April 1916: Evening

BREAKOUT

At 20.00 hours, the O'Rahilly and his platoon left the GPO. After opening a way through their own barricade on Henry Street, they moved slowly down the street. As they advanced through the darkened streets, the acrid stench of high explosives was still thick in the air. They darted forward, taking cover in doorways before moving in sections along to the next place of cover. At the corner of Moore Street, the group divided into two, with one half taking the left-hand side of the street and the other advancing down the right. The street was a menacing wall of gloom as the Volunteers fanned out and moved forward.

Unknown to the advancing Volunteers, the Sherwood Foresters had erected a barricade across the top of the street. The soldiers made ready, pulling back the bolts of their rifles and taking aim. As the shout of 'Fire!' was heard, the air was shattered with the demonic rattle of machine-gun and rifle fire which cut through the advancing Volunteers. Having only advanced twenty-five yards, the O'Rahilly was shocked to hear the thwack of British rounds striking his men. Dropping to the ground at the corner of Sampson's Lane, the O'Rahilly was joined by some of his men. Volunteer Henry Coyle was shot and killed as he attempted to find cover. He was twenty-eight years old and a slater by trade. He left behind a widow and a baby boy who was born after his death.

There was a lull in the firing as the machine-gunner stopped firing to change the magazine on his Lewis gun. Taking advantage of the situation, the O'Rahilly opened fire on the British position before rallying his men and rushing out into Moore Street. As he charged forward he was hit by a heavy and long burst of British machine-gun fire that sent him spiralling backwards. Mortally wounded, the officer crawled into cover at Sackville Place and, taking out his field notebook, wrote the following message to his wife:

Darling Nancy, I was shot leading a rush up Moore Street and took refuge in a doorway. While I was there I heard the men pointing me out where I was and made a bolt for the laneway I am in now. I got more [than] one bullet I think. Tons and tons of love dearie, to you and the boys and to Nell and Anna. It was a good fight anyhow. Please deliver this to Nannie O'Rahilly, 40 Herbert Park, Dublin. Goodbye, darling.[1]

He slowly began to bleed out and slipped into unconsciousness before succumbing to his wounds. The O'Rahilly was forty-one years old and a founding member of the Irish Volunteers. He was survived by his wife and five children.

Battleground

The remainder of the platoon, devoid of cover, was cut to pieces. Patrick Shortis was shot and killed during the advance on Moore Street. He was a native of Ballybunion, County Kerry. Volunteer Lieutenant Francis Macken was also shot down. He was twenty-four years old and resided in York Street, Dublin. Charles Carrigan, killed in the rush up Moore Street, was born in Glasgow of Irish parents and was killed on his thirty-fourth birthday. More than two-thirds of the platoon were killed or wounded as they attempted to break through the British lines. An attempt to outflank the machine gun by moving into Cole's Lane failed, and under the crushing fire, the remnants of the platoon, many of them wounded, were pinned down. Volunteer William Daly emptied the magazine of his rifle towards the British barricade before he was hit and wounded. The survivors managed to crawl back out of the line of fire and found refuge in a stable. Daly, like many others, applied the field dressing he carried to his wound and, exhausted from the loss of blood, soon fell asleep. The desultory sound of gunfire continued outside.

Behind the barricade on upper Moore Street, Captain G. J. Edmunds of the Sherwood Foresters ordered his men to cease fire. Covered by his colleagues, a sergeant moved out and carefully moved down Moore Street towards the body of the O'Rahilly. Rummaging through the officer's pockets, the sergeant retrieved the note the O'Rahilly had written to his wife and Connolly's last orders, which were immediately sent to General Maxwell. The regimental history records the discovery of the O'Rahilly's body:

We also found a letter written by the O'Rahilly to his wife after he was wounded, in which he said he was shot leading a charge. He got into an entry on the side of the street and in trying to escape from there he was shot again and killed – a brave man.[2]

Having given the O'Rahilly's recon force a forty-minute head-start, the main body of Volunteers, consisting of an estimated 350 men and three women, formed up in the GPO and at 20.40 hours made ready to evacuate. Pearse ordered his command to take as much food and ammunition as they could carry and make their way to the Williams and Woods factory on Great Britain Street. Ammunition and rations were handed out and stashed in packs, belts and bandoliers. As the inferno raged, the Volunteers formed up in small groups at the side entrance and made ready to leave GHQ. Volunteer Frank Burke later wrote:

> There was no panic whatsoever; we marched out two-deep, each man holding his rifle pointing upwards lest, in the closely packed formation, a rifle might go off accidentally. I remember well E. Bulfin was in front of me. When we reached the side door leading into Henry Street Commandant Pearse was standing in the small hallway watching and waiting until the last man had passed out of the building. As the street was being swept by machine-gun fire from Mary Street direction, we had to make a dash across in one's and two's into Henry Lane. I could see the bullets like hailstones hopping on the street and I thought that [it] would be a miracle to get to the other side scatheless. With head down as if running against heavy rain, I ran as I never ran before or since, and got

into Henry Lane without a scratch. The remarkable fact was that no one was hit while running this dangerous gauntlet.[3]

Moving fast and staying low, the Volunteers rushed across the street. Although the wounded had been evacuated earlier, there had been a number of casualties since then who had to be assisted across the bullet-swept street. James Connolly was carried on a stretcher and every undulation, every bump, caused his leg to move, triggering extreme pain. With bullets tearing through the air above them, the small groups scuttled along. Oscar Traynor described the scene in Henry Place:

> We crossed Henry Street under heavy fire and entered Henry Place. When we entered Henry Place there seemed to me to be a state bordering on chaos. Men were trying to get shelter in doorways and against walls from the fire, which no one seemed to know whence it was coming.[4]

Bullets tore up the ground at their feet as the Volunteers sought whatever cover they could.

Volunteer Arthur Weekes was shot dead. Originally from England, he had come to Ireland as a conscientious objector. He was noted for the IWW (Wobblies) badge he wore in his lapel.

Some of the Volunteers breeched an entry into O'Brien's Mineral Water Factory:

> James Connolly was being carried along on a stretcher. He was left down in the middle of the road and shouted out

what seemed to be orders. Some Volunteers attempted to break down a large door with their rifle butts, but in doing so shot three or four men who were behind them. Apparently the safety catches were off; they had been shaken off. Eventually a small man named John O'Connor (Blimey) persuaded some of the men to lift him and put him through a small window, after which he opened the door from inside.[5]

Shouted orders were obliterated by prolonged bursts of machine-gun fire. A few hundred yards away, shells impacted with a crash spouting up clouds of fire and dust.

The remainder of the group soon bunched up and were confronted by what they thought was an enemy strongpoint in the form of a small, whitewashed, one-storey slated house that was rushed by a section of Volunteers:

> We charged the building, entered it and found it unoc-cupied. What McLoughlin took to be fire from this building was in fact the splashes of plaster caused by the volume of machine gun fire which was crashing against the front of the house and which was being directed from the Rotunda Hospital in Parnell St. Cullen, who was with me when we entered the building, went out to the front to look into the front room and was hit on the leg and fell to the ground. We got Cullen back out of the line of fire.[6]

For more than an hour, the air vibrated and the earth rocked and shuddered. Through the sustained uproar of the shelling and the tap and rattle of machine guns, the Volunteers continued to secure the area and establish a defensive perimeter. Most of the doors in Moore Lane were locked and as the Volunteers attempted to fire through the lock, the bullet passed through the door, killing a girl and wounding her father. Attempts to evacuate the non-combatants were met with fierce resistance as the only alternative was braving the bullet-swept streets.

Outside, the fighting was confused and intense. Gunfire crackled across the town and the air was filled with the shrieks and groans of injured and dying. Volunteers and petrified civilians against a backdrop of exploding grenades, mortars and artillery shells. Many innocent men, women and children were shot down as they attempted to flee the battleground. An advance party battled their way to the end of Moore Lane and Henry Place and found the junction enfiladed by machine-gun fire.

Volunteer Michael Mulvihill was hit by a burst of machine-gun fire and killed. He was thirty-seven years old and originally from County Kerry. Tom Clarke rallied his men and, breaking into a store, the Volunteers wheeled out a dray and constructed a barricade across the street to block the fire. With the obstruction in place and providing some cover, the group managed to occupy a corner house at Moore Street and Moore Lane by boring a hole in an outer wall. Caked in dust and bathed in sweat, the Volunteers scrambled into the building. The exhausted men, their uniforms filthy, their skin blackened with powder, their eyes staring and their faces gaunt, sank to the ground and awaited further orders. Sixteen-year-old Volunteer John MacLoughlin rallied the Volunteers and ensured that they found cover in the streets. Impressed by the young man's vigour and qualities of leadership, James Connolly promoted the Volunteer to the rank of commandant. On receiving his commission he suggested the men get some rest and prepare for what the following morning might bring.

The group of Cumann na mBán and wounded that had left the GPO earlier that day found themselves taking cover in the Coliseum Theatre (G). Taking advantage of a lull in the shelling, they then moved out into the maelstrom that was Prince's Street and continued into Abbey Street. They navigated through the battleground for hours until the group came upon a sand-bagged British post on Jervis Street. Captain Orr of the Sherwood Foresters stepped forward and, with his drawn revolver, beckoned the group forward. After some negotiating the officer permitted the group to deposit their wounded in Jervis Street Hospital. While the male members of the group were taken under guard to Dublin Castle, the Cumann na mBán members were permitted to return home. The dishevelled group looked back towards Sackville Street and thought of their fellow Volunteers, cut off and surrounded, poised on the brink of annihilation.

Chapter 15

Saturday, 29 April 1916:
The Last Stand

As dawn broke, the fighting continued. No time was lost by the Volunteers as they consolidated their new position. From 11.00 hours on Friday night to 02.00 hours on Saturday morning, the Volunteers barricaded all the houses they had occupied by throwing furniture down the stairways into the bottom halls, blocking the doorways. Joe Good recalled the operation:

> By this time we had approximately 18 to 20 wounded men. Nearly all of these men were carried into the first house. We were considerably compressed in the small house, having not yet broken through into the other houses. James Connolly was carried up a narrow staircase. The staircase was so narrow that it was impossible to take him up the stairs until four strong men lifted him horizontally at extended arm's length over the banister rail.[1]

It was decided to break through the houses along the street. Groups of men with picks and sledgehammers began battering through the walls, moving from house to house. Shelling and machine-gun fire continued outside, with one shell demolishing a house at the lower part of Moore Street. Many of the Volunteers, exhausted, demoralised and suffering from combat fatigue, collapsed and slept on the floors with their rifles by their sides.

Nurse Elizabeth O'Farrell later wrote:

After breakfast, Mr Connolly and the other wounded men were carried through the holes [from No. 10], and all others followed. Mr Connolly was put to bed in a back room in [No.] 16 Moore Street. The members of the Provisional Government were in this room for a considerable length of time [P. H. Pearse, J. Connolly, J. Plunkett, T. Clarke, and Seán MacDermott] where they held a council of war. Willie Pearse was also with them.[2]

The officers had deep shadows around their eyes, their hair and uniforms were coated in thick plaster dust from the shelling. Any attempt to light a fire in order to cook some food attracted a barrage of rifle and machine-gun fire against the new Irish Command Post (CP). Throughout the morning, artillery fire boomed overhead, shaking the foundations of the buildings. Huge explosions emanated from the GPO, where the fires had reached the basement arsenal, sending up plumes of black smoke into the morning sky. The ground shuddered as the shock waves spread through the surrounding streets.

Not realising that the GPO had been vacated, British forces prepared for an all-out assault on the building. Colonel Hodgkin, commanding officer of the 2/6th Sherwood Foresters, summoned Captain G. J. Edmunds to their Battalion CP in Great Britain Street and ordered Hodgkin to take a platoon in support of Colonel Owens and the Royal Irish Regiment who were preparing to assault the GPO. Troops were amassing in the side streets for the final push against the Volunteer positions.

A breakout had to be formulated and a plan was devised to rush the British barricade on Moore Street. If the barricade was breached, the remainder of the garrison could push on to the Williams and Woods factory. A platoon was assembled under Captain George Plunkett, and as the bolt of the gate was being pushed back to allow the group out, a Volunteer rushed into the yard and ordered the men to stand down. The charge had been cancelled as the Irish commanders decided to treat with the British. After a period of deliberations, it was decided to surrender. Not all the commanders agreed with this course of action and many of the Volunteers voiced their disapproval at this decision. Volunteer Joe Good recalled the incident that set in motion the series of events for the surrender:

Sometime later that morning a party of civilians, mostly women, were attempting to leave from the other side of Moore Street. We received an order to cease fire, and this order was obeyed, though there was still considerable firing from the enemy positions. I thought that the British had agreed in some way to the evacuation of [the] women. Some men among the civilians had been warned not to go, but they persisted. I heard this order shouted by the enemy: 'Females advance and males stand'. Then there was a burst of fire. The women had managed to cross the street. But one man, at least, was riddled with bullets. He lay there on a white sheet, attached to a sweeping brush.[3]

At 12.45 hours, Nurse Elizabeth O'Farrell moved out into Moore Street holding aloft a white flag. Firing ceased as she made her way through the smoke and debris of battle towards the British barricade. On reaching the obstruction she was met by Colonel Hodgkin, who ordered that the nurse be escorted into Great Britain Street to meet with Colonel Portal. Having heard that the Irish Volunteers wanted to negotiate surrender, Portal telephoned Trinity College where General Lowe had established a field headquarters. General Lowe, accompanied by Captain H. de Courcy Wheeler, drove to Great Britain Street where Lowe stated that only an unconditional surrender would be accepted and that they had thirty minutes to decide. If this ultimatum was exceeded, hostilities would resume. Nurse O'Farrell reported this fact to Pearse, who discussed the matter with his fellow officers. Pearse attempted to negotiate with Lowe by sending Nurse O'Farrell back with a request for terms for his men but Lowe refused and insisted that if Pearse did not return with Nurse

O'Farrell and James Connolly on a stretcher, he would order his men to attack.

At 14.30 hours, Commander-in-Chief Patrick Pearse was met by General Lowe at the British barricade on Moore Street. As Pearse was removed by motor car to meet with General Maxwell at the Headquarters of Irish Command in Parkgate Street, Nurse O'Farrell was held under guard. Moments later, James Connolly was taken out on a stretcher and evacuated under guard to the Red Cross Hospital at Dublin Castle.

Driving through the city, Pearse viewed the devastation of Easter week. Buildings lay in ruins and fires burned furiously as thick smoke blackened the sky.

On arrival at British headquarters, Pearse was ushered before General Maxwell, where he agreed to an unconditional surrender of his forces. Pearse wrote:

> In order to prevent the further slaughter of Dublin citizens, and in the hope of saving the lives of our followers now surrounded and hopelessly outnumbered, the members of the Provisional Government present at headquarters have agreed to an unconditional surrender, and the Commandants of the various districts in the city and country will order their commands to lay down arms.
>
> (Signed) P. H. Pearse.
> 29th April, 1916, 3.45 p.m.[4]

The note was brought to Connolly at Dublin Castle, who endorsed the document with the words:

I agree to these conditions for the men only under my command in the Moore Street District and for the men in the St. Stephen's Green Command.

(Signed) James Connolly.

29/16[5]

Copies of the note were issued to Nurse Elizabeth O'Farrell, who was ordered to return to Moore Street along with details of how the garrison should surrender.

Carrying a white flag, proceed down Moore Street, turn into Moore Lane and Henry Place, out into Henry Street and around the pillar to the right hand side of Sackville Street. March up to 100 yards of the military drawn up at the Parnell Statue, halt, advance five paces and lay down arms.[6]

As the cacophony of battle died away and the smoke slowly cleared, the Volunteers moved out of their positions and into Moore Street. Here, they were greeted by the desolation of war as the dead and dying lay in the street. Around the street was scattered the detritus of battle: scraps of webbing, equipment, broken weapons, lumps of jagged shrapnel and fallen masonry.

Volunteer Thomas Leahy recalled:

Covered by their machine guns, we formed up as best we could after leaving our wounded sitting up at the side of the wall to be removed by Red Cross ambulance afterwards. We then turned into Henry Street

… under their orders and when we reached Nelson's Pillar and halted for a moment, we saw for the first time the state of the late H.Q. of the Republic – in ruins and still smouldering – and the remainder of that side all in the same condition. Again we got a reminder from the British to get moving and I need not here mention their typical language to us to do so. Both sides of the streets were lined with troops, five or six, with fixed bayonets, machine guns, artillery, and all forces at their command to receive our surrender. One of our group fixed a tricolour to his rifle and gave us the command 'Eyes right to the G.P.O.' before passing it.[7]

While other battalions were being informed of the surrender, the Volunteers of GHQ were marched to the grounds of the Rotunda Hospital where they were held in a small green area overnight. Those Volunteers that had held the defensive line to the rear of the GPO were taken under guard to St Mary's Abbey in Meeting House Lane and then transferred to Dublin Castle. The following day, Sunday, 30 April 1916, having fought with great bravery and élan, they were marched into captivity.

For the captured men, the end of the battle marked the conclusion of one story and the beginning of another. Of those arrested after the Rising, most were incarcerated in various British prisons: Knutsford, Lewes, Wandsworth, Wakefield, Stafford, Glasgow and Perth. Later, about 1,800 were transferred to an interment camp at Frongoch in Wales. The majority of the prisoners were released in August of

1916, the remainder in December. The convicted prisoners were freed in June 1917. Months of captivity would result in a reorganisation of the Irish Republican Army, with new strategies and tactics for a new war, one that would be bloodier than the Rising of 1916.

Chapter 16

Trial and Error

On 2 May 1916, Patrick Pearse was tried by Field General Court Martial at Richmond Barracks, Dublin. His charges read:

> Did an act to wit did take part in an armed rebellion and in the waging of war against His Majesty the King, such act being of such a nature as to be calculated to be prejudicial to the Defence to the Realm and being done with the intention and for the purpose of assisting the enemy.[1]

The prosecution called three witnesses: Lieutenant S. O. King of the Royal Inniskilling Fusiliers, Constable Daniel Coffey of the Detective Department of the Dublin Metropolitan Police and Sergeant G. Goodman of the Military Press at Staff Corps. The three men identified Pearse and linked him directly to the insurrection.

In his defence, Pearse did not call any witnesses but stated:

> My sole object in surrendering unconditionally was to save the slaughter of the civil population and to save

the lives of our followers who had been led into this thing by us. It is my hope that the British Government who has shown its strength will also be magnanimous and spare the lives and give an amnesty to my followers, as I am one of the persons chiefly responsible, have acted as C-in-C and president of the provisional Government. I am prepared to take the consequences of my act, but I should like my followers to receive an amnesty. I went down on my knees as a child and told God that I would work all my life to gain the freedom of Ireland. I have deemed it my duty as an Irishman to fight for the freedom of my country. I admit I have organised men to fight against Britain. I admit having opened negotiations with Germany. We have kept our word with her and as far as I can see she did her best to help us. She sent a ship with men. Germany has not sent us gold.[2]

The presiding judges, Brigadier General C. G. Blackadder (President), Lieutenant Colonel G. German and Lieutenant Colonel W. J. Kent found the accused guilty and passed the sentence of death. General Sir John Grenfell Maxwell confirmed the sentence.

On the morning of 3 May 1916, Patrick Pearse was escorted from his cell at Kilmainham Gaol to the stonebreakers yard. His hands were tied behind his back and a blindfold was secured over his eyes. As he was prepared for execution, the firing squad was marched into the yard and took up position, six soldiers kneeling and six standing. The squad had been drawn from the Nottingham and Derbyshire

Regiment, who had suffered the heaviest casualties during the fighting of Easter week. As the order to load, present, and fire was given, the sounds of the gunshots reverberated around the yard.

In the days that followed, the signatories of the Proclamation along with many of the senior officers of the republican army were executed at Kilmainham Gaol. They included Thomas MacDonagh, Thomas Clarke, Edward Daly, William Pearse, Michael Hanrahan, Eamonn Ceannt, Joseph Plunkett, John MacBride, Seán Heuston, Con Colbert, Michael Mallin and Seán Mac Diarmada. Apart from Thomas Kent, who was executed in Cork, all the executions took place within Kilmainham Gaol.

Due to his wounds, James Connolly's court martial was held on 9 May 1916 at the Red Cross Hospital, Dublin Castle. An extract from a memorandum concerning Connolly written by General Maxwell to Prime Minister Herbert. Asquith stated:

> This man has been a prominent leader in the Larkinite or Citizen Army for years. He was also a prominent supporter of the Sinn Féin movement.
>
> He held the rank of Commandant General of the Dublin Division in the rebel army, and had his headquarters at the G.P.O. from which place he issued orders. On the 24th April he issued and signed a general order to 'The officers and soldiers in Dublin of the Irish Republic' stating inter alia 'that the armed forces of the Irish Republic had everywhere met the enemy and defeated them.' This man was also a

signatory to the Declaration of Irish Independence already referred to.[3]

The prosecution produced a number of witnesses that verified Connolly's rank and his participation in the insurrection. Connolly stated:

I do not wish to make any defence except against charges of wanton cruelty to prisoners. These trifling allegations that have been made in that direction if they record facts that really happened deal only with the most unavoidable incidents of a hurried uprising, and overthrowing of long established authorities, and nowhere show evidence of a set purpose to wantonly injure unarmed prisoners.

We went out to break the connection between this country and the British Empire and to establish an Irish Republic.

We believe that the call we thus issued to the people of Ireland was a nobler call in a holier cause that [sic] any call issued to them during this war having any connection with the war.

We succeeded in proving that Irishmen are ready to die endeavouring to win for Ireland their national rights, which the British Government has been asking them to die to win for Belgium. As long as that remains the case the cause of Irish freedom is safe. Believing that the British Government has no right in Ireland, never had any right in Ireland, and never can have any right in Ireland, the presence in any one generation of even a respectable minority of Irishmen ready to die to affirm that truth makes that government for ever a[n] usurpation and a crime against human progress. I personally thank God that I have lived to see the day when thousands of Irishmen and boys, and hundreds of Irish women and girls, were equally ready to affirm that truth and seal it with their lives if necessary.[4]

The court martial found Connolly guilty and Colonel D. Sapte (President), Lieutenant Colonel A. M. Bent and Major F. W. Woodward sentenced the officer to death. The sentence, like all the others, was confirmed by General Maxwell.

In the early hours of 12 May 1916, James Connolly was taken from Dublin Castle by ambulance to the yard in Kilmainham Gaol. Because of his injuries he was seated in a chair before the firing squad. Father Aloysius suggested to Connolly that he should forgive the soldiers who would be responsible for his execution. Connolly replied, 'I respect every man who does his duty.'

Though the military would remain in control for the months that followed, the public outcry over the insurrection slowly turned to public sympathy for the Irish Volunteers. Defending his actions, General Maxwell wrote to Prime Minster Herbert Asquith, stating:

In view of the gravity of the rebellion and its connection with German intrigue and propaganda and in view of the great loss of life and destruction of property resulting therefrom, the General Officer, commanding in Chief, Irish Command, has found it imperative to inflict the most severe sentences on the known organisers of this detestable Rising and on those commanders who took an active part in the actual fighting which occurred. It is hoped that these examples will be sufficient to act as a deterrent to intrigues and to bring home to them that the murder of His Majesty's subjects or other acts calculated to imperil the safety of the realm will not be tolerated.[5]

On the same day as Connolly's execution, Asquith came to Ireland to see for himself the impact of the executions and the implementation of martial law. The prime minister supported Maxwell's course of action and defended him in Parliament. However, increasing pressure from the opposition and the Church to the executions slowly began to turn public opinion both in Ireland and in England.

Maxwell wrote to his wife, stating that, 'the first results of the punishments inflicted were good [...] The majority of people recognised that they were not excessive; but since then revulsion of feeling had set in'.[6] The officer predicted that as early as June 1916, if there were an election, Redmond's parliamentary party would be defeated and replaced by others perhaps less amenable to reason.[7]

Maxwell realised too late that the courts martial, the executions, the mass arrests and the deportations had marginalised the population and that the government and the military had lost their support because of his actions. As one act of defiance was brought to an end, another was just about to begin.

Chapter 17

Military Success and Military Failure

It is a well-known military axiom that no plan survives contact with the enemy. In the case of the 1916 Easter Rising, this truism is substantiated.

The military plan, devised by Plunkett and Connolly, called for the occupation of a number of positions within the city with an area of operations that covered 11km.

While the General Post Office (I) on Sackville Street was both the military and civil headquarters of the insurgents, it was not a fortress. This powerfully constructed stone building, commanding the main street of the city, was the communications centre for Ireland and England. By occupying this building, the insurgents were the precursors to the modern coup: throughout the twentieth century, television and radio stations were the main targets of occupation by revolutionary organisations. Though the GPO lacked adequate fields of fire, its location made it difficult for British artillery spotters to direct gunfire onto the position.

The countermanding order and the interception of the *Aud* greatly reduced the operational capabilities of the Irish Republican Army. The Dublin Brigade consisted of an estimated 3,000 Volunteers and the Citizen Army had a strength of approximately 400. On Easter Monday only 1,000 mustered with a further 800 reporting for duty later that week. By the end of Easter week the Headquarters Battalion at the GPO had 350 to 450 personnel fighting in the area. The insurgents showed remarkable military competence during a week of severe fighting. Though lacking in suitable weapons, the years of training in urban combat, the familiarity of their areas of operations and the high standard of the junior officers all contributed to a force that managed to withstand a week-long attack by one of the most powerful empires in the world.

Republican Headquarter staff were directing operations in a city that comprised two positions north and four positions south of the Liffey. The Headquarters Battalion established a perimeter defence, which provided protection for the Provisional Government at the GPO. However, the failure to occupy Trinity College left a gap between insurgent posts that the British exploited. Using Dame Street as a highway into the centre of the city and the college as a forwards-operations base, the British were able to deploy troops to the centre of the city.

The Irish Republican Army had a split command, with Pearse, the idealist, wholly committed to the cause of Irish independence and Connolly, the realist, who also believed in the cause of liberty but knew that his forces were outnumbered twenty to one.

Connolly realised by Tuesday morning that reinforcements were not coming to the city from the country and that his command stood alone. He remodelled his strategy to take this into account, redeploying his forces and strengthening his defences around GHQ. His theory that the British government would not permit the use of artillery to subdue an urban insurrection has often been criticised. (Connolly believed that the British capitalist class would never permit the deployment of artillery into a city in order to quell a rebellion.) The devastation of property caused by such an act would amount to millions of pounds. However, the British government did approve of the actions taken by the military and the centre of Dublin city was levelled, bringing the Rising to its conclusion. Captain Purcell, Chief of the Dublin Fire Brigade, submitted a report stating that 200 buildings had been destroyed with an approximate value of £2,500,000. The buildings that had stretched from Sackville Street along the right-hand side of Henry Street to Moore Street had been levelled. All that remained were piles of broken bricks, twisted iron and charred wood. The buildings that flanked the entrance to Cole's Lane had vanished. The destruction on the west side of Sackville Street included:

The whole block from the General Post Office back to Arnott's warehouse, fronting to Henry Street back to Prince's Street; the greater portion of the block from Sackville Street fronting to Lower Abbey Street back to Prince's Street and towards Liffey Street, within a short distance of the Independent Printing Office, where the fire was stopped; portion of the block to the south side of Middle Abbey Street, with two houses fronting to Sackville Street, up to and including No. 62 Middle

Abbey Street. This area of the fires on the west side of Sackville Street is 34,000 yards in extent.[1]

The total area burnt on the east side of Sackville Street consisted of:

Portions of the block between Cathedral Street and Earl Street, the whole block [of] Earl Street and Sackville Place, bounded by Nelson Lane at the back; portion of the block between Sackville Place and Abbey Street, the whole block between Abbey Street and Eden Quay, bounded by Marlborough Street on the east. The area of this east side district is 27,000 square yards.[2]

If Connolly had miscalculated the British army, so too did many others. Since 1914, Europe was witnessing a new type of warfare, one that encompassed mass shelling of cities with little or no regard for civilians or property. This new type of warfare was to develop as the century progressed.

Connolly's exit strategy was flawed, as the initial plan was to fall back to the Four Courts area and then to withdraw to north county Dublin. The failure to secure these egress routes resulted in both garrisons, that of the GPO and the Four Courts, becoming surrounded and isolated. A secure fallback position would have given the Volunteers just enough time to consolidate and defend themselves whilst they came up with an alternative solution to extricate the battalions from encirclement.

The British retaliated quickly to the evolving crisis, amassing a force of 20,000 troops within three days. As General Lowe deployed his troops into the city, he realised, with incidents at Mount Street and at the Mendicity Institute, that taking Dublin city was going to be bloodier than he initially thought. An urban fight is probably one of the toughest battles a commander can direct and when Lowe's initial sorties met tough resistance he was forced to rethink his tactical assault on the city. His deployment of machine guns at high vantage points throughout the city exploited the high ground, thus providing clear fields of fire. With the artillery, he used the weapon's capacity for indirect fire (firing out of sight of the enemy) to devastating effect. Using an arcing trajectory, the guns could fire over obstacles, hitting their targets. Similarly, his men used the trench mortars to devastating effect without exposing their positions. Armoured personnel carriers were used to great effect in order to gain a foothold in areas where the Volunteers were well entrenched. British troops were able to move fast and under cover to secure areas.

Many of the British troops in the Sackville Street area of operations had been fighting since Monday and the severe urban combat was unprecedented in the history of the British army. Never before had troops been engaged in such combat conditions and the racing through buildings, the sudden fire-fights, the constant incoming bullets and the smoke, mayhem and confusion of fighting in an urban battlefield had taken their toll. Private William Harold King of the 2/8th Sherwood Foresters later wrote:

In a very few days we hope to be there [France]. Personally I'm not particularly anxious to go (I think no one is). I have quite as much as I want in Dublin, but I am prepared, like most of us, to go quite cheerfully, and leave the outcome on the knees of the Gods.[3]

Initially, the British were forced to fight for every street corner and suffered heavy casualties. But with Lowe's change in tactics, he reduced the number of casualties that may have been suffered.

Operating in such a hostile environment, with thousands of civilians living within the area of operations, the British troops and the Irish Volunteers fought daily battles that gradually took their toll, both physically and mentally. Many of those soldiers that survived Easter week in Dublin would, in the coming months, be once again plunged into battle, this time at the Somme in France in July 1916.

CONCLUSION

The 1916 Easter Rising was a brief and bloody affair, fought on an urban battleground. For six days, 1,500 men, women and young boys and girls fought against a force of 20,000 British troops. As the military amassed around them, the beleaguered republican forces faced the inevitable hour and rushed headlong into the crucible of history.

Though the 1916 Rising is a pivotal point in our nation's history, the event is still a topic of controversy today. Those that planned and participated in the insurrection did not have a democratic mandate from the people to carry out an armed uprising against British rule in Ireland. Academics and historians have disagreed in their interpretation of its significance, their opinions more often than not influenced as much by their own political leanings as by knowledge of the subject. Regardless of how one interprets the impact of the Rising, there can be no doubt that the actions of Easter week 1916 and the events that followed are crucial to our understanding of the history and political development of modern Ireland. These facts can be disputed and the interpretations debated, but all this is incidental to the essential truth of the insurrection.

Paul O'Brien

As the final shots echoed throughout the stonebreakers yard in Kilmainham Gaol, the blood sacrifice of those who participated in the Rising elevated a minor military encounter into an epic battle for Irish freedom.

While other attempts at gaining independence became footnotes in the history books, storytellers, artists and historians reshaped the story of the Rising. It is perhaps Pearse's overall strategic plan – that of renewing the ideal of an independent Irish Republic – which became the greatest legacy of the 1916 Volunteers.

Endnotes

Foreword
1 Wills, C., *Dublin 1916 The Siege of the GPO* (Profile Books, London, 2009) p. 7.

Chapter 1
1 Molony, H., Witness Statement W/S 391 (Bureau of Military History 1913–21, Dublin).
2 O' Brien, P., *Uncommon Valour: 1916 & The Battle for the South Dublin Union* (Mercier Press, Cork, 2010).
3 Good, J., Witness Statement W/S 388 (Bureau of Military History 1913–21, Dublin).
4 Heuston, J. M., Headquarters Battalion Easter Week 1916.
5 Robinson, S., Witness Statement W/S 1721 (Bureau of Military History 1913–21, Dublin).
6 *Ibid.*
7 *Ibid.*
8 Caulfield, M., *The Easter Rebellion,* (Gill & MacMillan, Dublin, 1995) p. 8.

Chapter 2
1 Jeffery, K., *The GPO & The Easter Rising,* (Irish Academic Press, Dublin, 2006) p. 17.
2 Staines, M., Witness Statement W/S 284 (Bureau of Military History 1913–21, Dublin).

3   Brennan-Whitmore, W. J., *Dublin Burning: The Easter Rising from Behind the Barricades* (Mercier Press, Cork, 2013) p. 50.

4   Cremen, M., Witness Statement W/S 903 (Bureau of Military History 1913–21, Dublin).

Chapter 3

1   Hannant, A.C., PRO 75/92/1.

2   Soughley, M., Witness Statement W/S 189 (Bureau of Military History 1913–21, Dublin).

3   Ryan, D., Witness Statement W/S 724 (Bureau of Military History 1913–21, Dublin).

4   O Leary, J., Witness Statement W/S 1108 (Bureau of Military History 1913–21, Dublin).

5   McCabe, K., Witness Statement W/S 926 (Bureau of Military History 1913–21, Dublin).

Chapter 4

1   Brennan-Whitmore, W. J., *Dublin Burning: The Easter Rising from Behind the Barricades,* (Mercier Press, Cork, 2013) p. 98.

2   Thorton, F., Witness Statement W/S 510 (Bureau of Military History 1913–21, Dublin).

3   Brennan-Whitmore, *Dublin Burning: The Easter Rising from Behind the Barricades,* p. 63.

Chapter 5

1   Tannam, L., Witness Statement W/S 242 (Bureau of Military History 1913–21, Dublin).

2   Heron, A., Witness Statement W/S 293 (Bureau of Military History 1913–21, Dublin).

3   Bulfin, E., Witness Statement W/S 497 (Bureau of Military History 1913–21, Dublin).

4   Murphy, F., Witness Statement W/S 370 (Bureau of Military History 1913–21, Dublin).

5   Jeffery, K., *The GPO & the Easter Rising,* (Irish Academic Press, Dublin, 2006) p. 18.
6   Bradbridge, E. U., *59th Division 1915-1918* (Wilfred Edmunds, Chesterfield, 1928).

Chapter 6
1   Bateson, *They Died by Pearse's Side* (Irish Grave Publications, Dublin, 2010) p. 195.
2   *Ibid.,* p. 196.
3   *Ibid.,* p. 197.
4   Kildea, J., *Anzacs & Ireland,* (Cork University Press, Cork, 2007) pp. 63–64.
5   *Ibid.,* p. 52.

Chapter 7
1   Jeffrey, K., *The G.P.O. and the Easter Rising* (Irish Academic Press, Dublin, 2006) p. 144.
2   Ryan, D., Witness Statement W/S 724 (Bureau of Military History 1913–21, Dublin).
3   Macauley, C. J., Witness Statement W/S 735 (Bureau of Military History 1913–21, Dublin).
4   Traynor, O., Witness Statement W/S 340 (Bureau of Military History 1913–21, Dublin).
5   Connolly, J. 25th April 1916.
6   Colgan, P., Witness Statement W/S 850 (Bureau of Military History 1913–21, Dublin).
7   Leahy, T., Witness Statement W/S 660 (Bureau of Military History 1913–21, Dublin).
8   Knightly, M., Witness Statement W/S 834 (Bureau of Military History 1913–21, Dublin).

Chapter 8
1   Brennan-Whitmore, W. J., *Dublin Burning: The Easter Rising from Behind the Barricades* (Mercier Press, Cork, 2013) pp. 98–99.

2   Traynor, O., Witness Statement W/S 340 (Bureau of Military History
    1913–21, Dublin).

Chapter 9

1   Caulfield, M., *The Easter Rising* (Gill & MacMillan, Dublin, 1995) p. 139.
2   Traynor, O., Witness Statement W/S 340 (Bureau of Military History
    1913–21, Dublin).
3   *Ibid.*

Chapter 10

1   T. Dore, E., Witness Statement W/S 153 (Bureau of Military History
    1913–21, Dublin).
2   Traynor, O., Witness Statement W/S 340 (Bureau of Military History
    1913–21, Dublin).
3   McCabe, K., Witness Statement W/S 926 (Bureau of Military History
    1913–21, Dublin).
4   Thornton, F., Witness Statement W/S 615 (Bureau of Military History
    1913–21, Dublin).

Chapter 11

1   Nunan, S., Witness Statement W/S 1744 (Bureau of Military History
    1913–21 , Dublin).
2   Bateson, R., *They Died by Pearse's Side* (Irish Graves Publications, Dublin,
    2010) p. 170.
3   Foy. M., & Barton. B., *The Easter Rising,* (Sutton Publishing,
    Gloucestershire, 2006) p.191.
4   Bradbridge, E.U., 59th *Division 1915-1918* (Wilfred Edmunds,
    Chesterfield, 1928).
5   Saurin, C., Witness Statement W/S 288 (Bureau of Military History
    1913–21, Dublin).

Chapter 12

1   Caulfeld, M., *The Easter Rebellion,* (Gill & Macmillan, Dublin, 1996) p. 247.

2 Bridger, G., *The Great War Handbook,* (Pen & Sword, Barnsley, 2009) p. 128.
3 Oates, W. C., *The 2/8th Battalion, The Sherwood Foresters in the Great War* (J&H Bell Ltd., Nottingham, 1921).
4 Heenan, G. F. H., PRO 67/196/1.
5 Woods, W., PRO 32/18/27.

Chapter 13
1 Bulfin, E., Witness Statement W/S 497 (Bureau of Military History 1913–21, Dublin).
2 Harris, T., Witness Statement W/S 320 (Bureau of Military History 1913–21, Dublin).
3 McGarry, F., *Rebels, Voices from the Easter Rising,* (Penguin, Dublin, 2011) p. 236.
4 Beazley, F., PRO 2/7/28.
5 Good, J., Witness Statement W/S 388 (Bureau of Military History 1913–21, Dublin).

Chapter 14
1 Bateson, R., *They Died by Pearse's Side* (Irish Graves Publications, Dublin, 2010) p. 170.
2 Oates, W. C., *The 2/8th Battalion, The Sherwood Foresters in the Great War* (J&H Bell Ltd., Nottingham, 1921).
3 McGarry, F., *Rebels, Voices from the Easter Rising,* (Penguin, Dublin, 2011) p. 238.
4 Traynor, O., Witness Statement W/S 340 (Bureau of Military History 1913–21, Dublin).
5 Good, J., Witness Statement W/S 388 (Bureau of Military History 1913–21, Dublin).
6 Traynor, O., Witness Statement W/S 340.

Chapter 15
1 Good, J., Witness Statement W/S 388 (Bureau of Military History 1913–21, Dublin).

2 O' Farrell, E., *The Story of the 1916 Surrender* (The Workers Party, Dublin,1981).
3 Good, J., Witness Statement W/S 388.
4 O' Farrell, *The Story of the 1916 Surrender.*
5 *Ibid.*
6 *Ibid.*
7 Leahy, T., Witness Statement W/S 660 (Bureau of Military History 1913–21, Dublin).

Chapter 16
1 PRO WO71/345.
2 PRO WO71/345.
3 Barton, B., *From Behind a Closed Door* (The Blackstaff Press, Belfast, 2002) p. 280.
4 *Ibid.,* p. 297.
5 *Ibid.,* p. 63.
6 *Ibid.,* p. 87.
7 *Ibid.,* p. 87.

Chapter 17
1 Fallon, L., *Dublin Fire Brigade & the Irish Revolution* (South Dublin Libraries, Dublin, 2012) pp. 115–131.
2 *Ibid.*
3 Mansfield & North Notts Advertiser 19th May 1916.

Select Bibliography

Bateson, R., *They Died by Pearse's Side* (Irish Grave Publications, Dublin, 2010)

Barton, B., *From Behind a Closed Door* (The Blackstaff Press, Belfast, 2002)

Brennan-Whitmore, W.J., *Dublin Burning, The Easter Rising from Behind the Barricades* (Mercier Press, Cork, 2013)

Bradbridge, E.U., *59th Division 1915-1918* (Wilfred Edmunds,Chesterfield, 1928)

Caulfield, M., *The Easter Rebellion* (Gill & MacMillan, Dublin, 1995)

Fallon, L., *Dublin Fire Brigade & the Irish Revolution* (South Dublin Libraries, Dublin, 2012)

Jeffery, K., *The GPO & The Easter Rising* (Irish Academic Press, Dublin, 2006)

Kildea, J., *Anzacs & Ireland* (Cork University Press, Cork, 2007)

O'Farrell, E., *The Story of the 1916 Surrender* (The Workers Party, Dublin,1981)

Oates, W.C., *The 2/8th Battalion, The Sherwood Foresters in the Great War* (J&H Bell Ltd, Nottingham, 1921)

Wills, C., *Dublin 1916 The Siege of the GPO* (Profile Books, London, 2009)

INDEX

3rd Reserve Cavalry Brigade 19, 45
59th North Midland Division 42, 68, 84
5th Reserve Artillery Brigade 19
Dublin University Officers Training Corps 28

Allatt, Colonel Henry T.W. 66
Alton, Captain E.H. 28
Amiens Street 27, 28, 32, 33, 41, 58, 60, 85
Annesley Bridge 57
Annesley Place 29
ANZACs 44, 47, 61
Arnott and Co. 32
Aston Quay 48
Athlone 19, 55, 59
Aud 3, 7, 122

Bachelors Walk 17, 30, 53
Ballybough Bridge 29
Bent, Lieutenat Colonel A.M. 119
Beresford Place 7, 12, 59
Bewley Sons 32

Birrell, Augustine 41
Blackadder, General C.G. 116
Blanchardstown 55
Boland, Mick 70
Boland's flour mills 17
Bourke, David, 34
Bracken, Peader
Bulfin, Eamon 13, 64
Burke, Frank 102
Byrne, Tom 37

Capel Street 32, 58, 72, 78, 79, 85
Carlisle Bridge 22, 30, 74, 89
Carney, Winnie 13
Carrigan, Charles 101
Casement, Roger 3
Ceannt, Eamonn 9, 10, 17, 117
Chalmers, A.D. 13
City Hall 37, 41, 46
Clarke, Liam 39
Clarke, Thomas 9, 10, 17, 117
Clarke's Bridge 28
Clery's/Imperial Hotel 31, 34, 65, 74

Cole's Lane 85, 101, 123
Colgan, Patrick 54, 82
Coliseum Theatre 32, 95, 106
Collins, Michael 10, 13, 15
Connaught Rangers 18
Connolly, Seán 12
Connolly, James 3, 4, 9, 12, 21, 52, 63, 65, 71, 103, 106, 107, 111, 112, 117, 119
Conroy, Andrew 49
Coyle, Henry 100
Crawford, George 43
Cremen, Michael 20
Crofts, Gerald 36
Crown Alley 41, 18
Cumann na Mbán 7, 17, 39, 62, 95, 106
Curragh 19, 42, 46
Custom House 27, 53, 58, 59, 60, 85, 90, 91

D'Olier Street 53, 55, 61, 64, 69, 89
Daly, Edward 11, 117
Daly, William 53, 101
De Valera, Eamon 17
Denmark Street 72, 85, 86
Dore, Eamon 71
Drumcondra 57
Dublin Bread Company 36, 52, 61, 65, 82
Dublin Castle 12, 17, 19, 27, 28, 41, 46, 47, 58, 68, 77, 78, 85, 106, 111, 113, 117, 119
Dublin Metropolitan Police 22, 24, 115

Dublin Wireless School of Telegraphy 34
Dunphy, Edward 24

Eason's 31, 32, 64
Eden Quay 13, 30, 53, 124
Edmunds, Captain G.J. 101, 109
Ennis, Peter 60
Exchange Hotel 37

Fianna Éireann 7, 17
Fitzgerald, Desmond 18, 50
Fleet Street 31
Four Courts 11, 17, 41, 46, 58, 68, 78, 79, 89, 124
Freemans Journal 63

Gardiner Street 58, 85
German, Lieutenant Colonel G. 116
Glasnevin 27, 56
Gleeson, Joseph 24
Glen, James 45
Gloucester Street 75
Good, Joe 11, 53, 107, 109
Grattan Bridge 78, 79
Great Brunswick Street 59, 70
Grennan, Julia 95
Gresham Hotel 55, 62, 66, 67, 80
Gutherie, Samuel 15

HMS *Helga* 59, 61
Hammond, Colonel 22, 23
Harris, G.A. 28
Harris, Tom 93

Heenan, G.F.H. 87
Henderson, Frank 31, 75
Henry Street 20, 31, 32, 72, 73, 88,
    97, 98, 99, 102, 103, 112, 123
Heron, Aine 38
Heuston, Seán 11, 117
Hibernian Bank 35, 38, 61
Hibernian Rifles 37
Hodgkin, Colonel 109, 110
Hopkins and Hopkins 30, 48, 49,
    60, 61, 64, 65, 82
Hoyte's Chemist 82
Humphries, Dick 81

Irish Citizen Army (ICA) 3, 7, 8, 9,
    12, 17, 81
Irish Republican
    Brotherhood (IRB) 3, 7, 9, 10
Irish Times 35, 68
Irish Volunteers 46, 100, 110, 119,
    126

Jacob's Biscuit Factory 10, 17
Jervis Street 18, 24, 40, 81, 85, 95,
    106
Johnson, Francis 1

Keely, John 24
Kelly, James 55
Kelly's Gunpowder store (Kelly's
    Fort) 30
Kent, Colonel W.J. 116
Keogh, Gerald 43
Kilmainham Gaol 116, 117, 119, 128
Kingsbridge Station 19, 26, 46

Kingstown 19, 58
Knightly, Michael 32, 55

Leahy, Thomas 19, 26, 46
Leinster Avenue 29
Leinster Regiment 59
Liberty Hall 7, 8, 9, 10, 11, 12, 24,
    59, 60
Liffey Street 32, 72, 73, 79, 123
Lowe, W.H.M. 4, 19, 45, 46, 47, 58,
    59, 67, 77, 84, 110, 111, 125
Lower Abbey Street 13, 32, 34, 35,
    52, 53, 61, 68, 72, 89, 123
Lower Britain Street 58

Mac Diarmada (MacDermott)
    Seán 9, 11, 28, 59, 65, 125
MacInerney & Co. 32
Macken, Francis 101
MacNeill, Eoin 3, 5
Magazine Fort 17, 27
Mahony, Captain George 57, 58
Mallin, Michael 12, 17, 117
Manfield's Boot Store 60
Marlborough Barracks 22, 27
Mary Street 72, 102
Maxwell, General Sir John
    Grenfell 84, 116
Maynooth 37
McBirney's 48, 49
McCabe, Kevin 74
McDonagh, Thomas 9, 10, 17,
    117
McGinly, Billy 58
McLoughlin, Dan 39

Meeting House Lane 113

Mendicity Institute 11, 28, 59, 65, 125

Metropole Hotel 13, 31, 53, 58, 73, 74, 88, 89

Molony, Helena 8

Moore Lane 105, 112

Moore Street 80, 96, 97, 99, 100, 101, 105, 108, 109, 110, 111, 112, 123

Morrough, Major J.D. 70

Mulvihill, Michael 105

Murphy, William Martin, 34

Nathan, Sir Matthew 41

Nelson's Pillar 2, 40, 113

Noblett's 25, 33

North Earl Street 23, 32, 33, 53, 76, 90

North Strand 29

North Wall 27, 28

Norway, Hamilton 1

Norway, Mary Louisa 1

Nunan, John 40

O'Flanagan, Fr John 39

O'Kelly Fergus 34

O'Connell, Daniel 2

O'Connor John (Blimey) 24, 35, 104

O'Connor, Patrick 75

O'Farrell, Elizabeth 11, 53, 107, 109

O'Leary, Jeremiah 25

O'Neill's Public House 72, 86

O'Rahilly 11, 12, 16, 55, 73, 94, 97, 98, 99, 100, 101, 102

O'Reilly, Thomas 81

Owens, Colonel 109

Parliament Street 37, 78

Parnell Square 80

Parnell, Charles Stewart 2, 22

Pearse, Patrick 9, 21, 111, 115, 116

Phoenix Park 17, 27

Pillar Café 33

Plunkett, George 9, 80, 109

Plunkett, Jack 40

Plunkett, Joseph 4, 9, 10, 13, 34, 51, 117

Poole, Vincent 60

Portal, Colonel 46, 110

Power, Nancy Wyse 80

Prince's Street 20, 24, 31, 63, 73, 96, 106, 123

Purcell, Captain 38, 39, 123

Rathfarnham 24

Reid, John 72

Reis's and Co. 34

Richmond Barracks 115

Robinson, Séamus 12, 13, 30

Royal Canal 27, 28

Royal Dublin Fusiliers 19, 28, 56

Royal Hospital Kilmainham 84

Royal Inniskilling Fusiliers 115

Royal Irish Regiment 60, 66, 69, 79, 85, 96, 109

Russell, Seán 60

Ryan, James 39, 72

Sackville Street 2, 3, 4, 8, 13, 22, 25, 27, 31, 33, 35, 46, 47, 53, 55, 57, 58, 60, 61, 62, 64, 66, 68, 70, 71, 76, 79, 81, 82, 88, 89, 95, 96, 106, 112, 121, 124, 125
Sandbach, Major General A.E. 42
Sapte, Colonel D. 119
Shields, Arthur 35
Shortis, Patrick 101
Skeffington, Francis Sheehy 26
Soughley, Michael 24
South Dublin Union 10, 17
Spring Garden Street 29
St Stephen's Green 12, 17, 46, 112
St Mary's Abbey 113
Staines, Michael 18
Sweeny, Joe 67

Talbot Street 15
Tannam, Liam 37, 70

Thornton, Frank 9, 31, 34
Traynor, Oscar 31, 52, 60, 64, 69, 73, 89, 103
Trinity College 4, 28, 31, 43, 46, 47, 49, 58, 60, 68, 81, 85, 110, 122
Turner, Cormac 48

Ulster Volunteer Force 2, 3

Viceregal Lodge 27

Waverly Hotel 82
Weafer, Tom 28
Weekes, Arthur 103
Westmorland Street 48, 53, 61, 69, 88
Whitmore, W.J. Brennan 10, 17, 32
Woods, James W. 87
Woodward, Major F.W. 119
Wynn's Hotel 68